# Parties, Elections, and Representation in the State of New York

## Howard A. Scarrow

New York University Press
New York and London
1983

Copyright © 1983 by New York University

Library of Congress Cataloging in Publication Data

Scarrow, Howard A.
  Parties, elections, and representation in the
state of New York.

  Includes bibliographical references and indexes.
  1. Political parties—New York (State)  2. Elections
—New York (State)  3. Apportionment (Election law)—
New York (State)  I. Title.
JK2295.N73S27  1983      324.6′09747      83-2147
ISBN 0-8147-7828-3
ISBN 0-8147-7829-1 (pbk.)


Clothbound editions of New York University Press book are Smyth-
sewn and printed on permanent and durable acid-free paper.




Manufactured in the United States of America

# Contents

# Preface

POLITICAL PARTIES, elections, and the system of representation in which they operate constitute the most vital components of democratic government. They are what distinguish democracies from authoritarian regimes. Comparative analysis has shown, however, that these components vary significantly from one democratic country to another and from one American state to another. It is the purpose of this volume to depict the features of parties, elections, and the system of representation as these exist, or have existed, in the state of New York.

Three major perspectives have guided the analysis. The first is comparison with other American states. It is not enough for the student of politics to know what the political practices in New York are. Just as important, the student should know how these practices resemble or differ from those in other states. A comparative perspective is especially appropriate when looking at New York, where many practices are, or have been in the past, distinctive. These include practices relating to primary elections, cross endorsement, voter registration, and apportionment formulas.

The second perspective of the analysis is historical evolution. Contemporary political practices in New York differ not only from those in other American states, but differ also from practices in the New York of previous generations. Primary elections are less than a century old, the challenge primary fifteen years old, and the four-year registration period less than a year old at the time of writing. Today's free-for-all primaries and today's low voter turnout are relatively new phenomena. Tracking political evolution and explaining it constitute a major focus of each of the chapters which follow.

A third and related perspective of the analysis is the question of political outcome and how outcome is related to intent. What consequences have resulted from the adoption in New York of the "one man, one vote" principle of representation? The adoption of the Wilson-Pakula Law? The adoption of permanent voter registration? Were these results the ones intended or hoped for by the courts? By the state legislature? By the reformers? A theme which unites the chapters is the conclusion that they were not.

A fourth perspective which has guided the analysis stems from the absence of a volume which focuses on parties and elections in New York State as a whole. The bibliography of a widely used text on political parties and elections in the American states, published in 1982, lists six separate entries for the state of California and at least three entries each for the states of Massachusetts, Minnesota, Pennsylvania, Texas, and Virginia. Altogether there are entries for twenty states. Not one of these relates to the state of New York.[1] Accordingly, the present volume is cast in a statewide perspective, with only minimum attention given to the state's most conspicuous political unit, New York City. The politics of the City is a subject unto itself, as illustrated by such excellent, though now dated, works as Wallace Sayre and Herbert Kaufman's *Governing New York City* (1965), Edward Costikyan's *Behind Closed Doors* (1966), and relevant portions of James Q. Wilson's *The Amateur Democrat* (1962).

The methodology which characterizes each chapter is a heavy reliance on aggregate data: election results, registration and enrollment data, and population data. The analysis is thus more in the tradition of the late V. O. Key, Jr., than it is of much contemporary political science literature, which relies heavily on the results of sample surveys. Care has been taken to focus only on subjects for which aggregate data provide a suitable basis for analysis and to avoid analysis of individual voter behavior, for which they do not. The reader who hopes to find the answers to questions such as how do WASPs vote, how do Jews vote, or how do Italian-Americans vote, will be disappointed.

A related disclaimer is in order. It is only because there have appeared many excellent journalistic accounts focusing on these and other questions concerning politics in New York State that the present volume, which is deliberately narrowly focused, is practical. The volume is thus intended to supplement and not to duplicate such works and Warren Moscow's dated but still valuable *Politics in the Empire State* (1948), or the relevant portions of Susan and

Martin Tolchin's *To the Victors* (1971), or Neal R. Peirce's *The Megastates* (1972).

Any author who writes from an historical perspective about politics in New York State owes a heavy debt to *The New York Times* for chronicling the historical record and for making that record usable through a published index and to the state of New York for publishing the periodic *Legislative Manual* containing detailed election results and other useful political information. Without these sources this volume could not have been written. The author also wishes to acknowledge the assistance received from the State Board of Elections and from the various county boards of election for supplying election data not contained in the *Manual*. For helping to stimulate the ideas contained in chapters five and six, and for allowing portions of a jointly-authored article to be reprinted, the author wishes to acknowledge his debt to Professor Bernard Grofman of the University of California, Irvine. Finally, for cheerfully typing the various drafts of the manuscript Mrs. Anne Giles and Ms. Shelly Gougler of the Department of Political Science at the State University at Stony Brook deserve special thanks.

The final editing of this volume took place at the time of the November 2, 1982 gubernatorial election. All of the major outcomes produced by that election and the preceding primary have been incorporated. However, the tables and other detailed analysis cover only the period through 1980.

## Note

1. Malcolm Jewell and David Olson, *American State Political Parties and Elections,* Revised Edition, The Dorsey Press (Homewood, Ill., 1982).

# 1.

# Parties
# and the Party System
# in the State of New York

POLITICAL PARTIES in the state of New York may be seen as (1) legitimate institutions of governance, (2) organizations of activists, (3) groups of supporters within the electorate, and (4) cohesive groups of legislators. At the same time, the system which they comprise may be designated a (5) multi-party system and a (6) competitive party system. This chapter, providing the framework for the remainder of the volume, will discuss each of these topics in turn.

## Parties as Legitimate Institutions of Governance

Less than a century ago political parties in New York State were completely private organizations. No less than churches, social clubs, and fraternal orders, political parties were detached from government and unregulated by government. Two developments in the 1890s transformed parties into what they are today: legitimate institutions participating in the process of government and institutions constrained by government regulation.

*Official Parties: Ballot Access*
The first of these developments was the introduction of the official ballot. Prior to legislation enacted in 1890 the folded paper the

voter dropped into the ballot box on election day was not a ballot in today's sense of the term; rather it was the printed list of a party's candidates, prepared by the party itself and made available by the party on election day. The change in 1890 to an official ballot printed at public expense was intended to make all the parties' ballots uniform in color and shape (the single-sheet ballot with all the parties' candidates—i.e., the Australian ballot—was not introduced until 1895), thus helping to insure secrecy of voting and helping to prevent voting fraud.

In enacting this reform, however, the lawmakers were forced to define what they meant by political parties, i.e., those organizations which were to be privileged to have the names of their candidates printed on the official ballot. The 1890 law, then, introduced the idea of an "officially recognized" party, and defined such a party as one which in the last election had polled at least one percent of the vote (for a statewide, district, or local office, depending on the office for which the ballot was being prepared). Such an organization could have its ballot (i.e., its list of candidates) printed at public expense and officially made available on election day. An organization not qualifying as a political party, as well as a single individual, could have a ballot officially printed and made available only by gathering a specified number of signatures on a petition (e.g., 1,000 signatures for a statewide office). If that petition effort failed, such candidates could be elected only if voters took the trouble of writing in their names on one of the official ballots. With this law, then, New York recognized that political parties serve the valuable purpose of reducing the number of choices before the electorate and that only those parties which have been shown to have some minimum basis of support should be encouraged. Other groups should have to expend effort to gain a ballot position.

Today the requirement for official party recognition has been changed to 50,000 votes polled by the party's gubernatorial candidate. What has not changed, however, has been the relative advantage of ballot access enjoyed by parties which have gained official status. Thus today an official party can have its candidates for the various statewide offices included on the official November ballot simply by submitting the names to the secretary of state; in contrast, the name of an independent, or the candidate of a non-official party, can appear only if 20,000 petition signatures (properly distributed throughout the state) are submitted. Below the statewide level the advantage enjoyed by official parties is not as great as it is for statewide office; since 1913 *all* candidates have had to gather petition signatures of one sort or another in order to gain access to the ballot. Yet even for these offices the number of signatures required for non-official contenders is three times the number required of contenders from the official parties.[1] Moreover, to make the task facing the non-official candidate more difficult, the election law stipulates that no one who has participated in an official party's primary election can sign such a petition. The county election boards, furthermore, whose top officials are appointed by the two largest parties, will often do everything they can legally to hinder a successful petition effort by a non-official candidate. To make the ballot advantage of the official parties still greater, the most favored ballot positions—the top lines (or the first columns) on today's voting machine—have always been reserved for them. Non-official candidates have had to be satisfied with lower ballot placement.

The pattern of growth and decline of New York's minor parties during this century—there have been 12—confirms the advantage derived from official party status. A party will begin by running a candidate for governor in order to obtain official status. Then, once official status has been obtained, virtually a full slate of candidates will be fielded in the following election. Finally, following the election in which the party's gubernatorial vote falls below the required minimum, the party disappears completely. New York's newest party, Right to Life, began the cycle in 1978, putting up a candidate only for governor. The candidate urged her supporters to cast a vote for her not because she was given a chance of winning the election, but because 50,000 votes were all she needed for her party to be given future access to the ballot. By 1979, the new party was contesting local offices throughout the state.

*Official Party Candidate Selection*
The second development in the 1890s which led to the transformation of political parties into the semi-public institutions they are today was the primary election legislation enacted in 1898. As will be discussed more fully in the next chapter, this legislation was designed to curb abuses in the parties' procedures for selecting

their candidates for public office. As such, the legislation was not welcomed by the parties. Nor was the state anxious to include many organizations in its scope since the law entailed administrative costs. For the purposes of this legislation, then, the definition of a political party was more stringent than it was for ballot access: an organization which had run a candidate for governor in the last gubernatorial election and whose candidate had polled at least 10,000 votes. Such an organization would now be forced to select its nominees in the manner prescribed by the law (i.e., the indirect primary method). For over 20 years there remained the dual standard for defining a political party—one standard for granting ballot access and another, more stringent, standard for regulating nominations. In 1922 the two standards were merged into one: an official political party for both purposes was defined as one whose gubernatorial candidate in the last election polled a specified minimum number of votes. As indicated above, today that figure is 50,000.

*Official Party Membership and Organization*
In order to confine participation in the newly formulated nominating procedures to persons who were party members, the 1898 lawmakers were forced to specify who those persons were. Accordingly, they defined a party member as one who declared loyalty to the party before the local election board and, thereby, "enrolled" in that party. The party organizations were thus provided with a publicly financed secretarial service that would keep up-to-date records of their membership. Throughout most of this century at least 90 percent of New York's registered voters have chosen to become enrolled members in one of the parties.

The 1898 law also specified the structure of the parties' organization: each party would have as its basic organizational unit the county committee. The law also laid down rules which the organizations had to follow in managing their affairs, such as that when a party held a convention, delegates had to be apportioned among the units of representation according to the party's strength as reflected in the last gubernatorial vote. Finally, and most important, the law provided that the party activists, i.e., the members of the county committees, would be chosen at the annual primary elections by the rank-and-file members. The newly established primary elections would thus serve not only the purpose of allowing party members to participate in the selection of the parties' nominees for public office, but would also serve the purpose of allowing them to select the persons who would run the party organizations. The publicly financed election machinery was thus given over to the parties so that they could choose their leadership in an ordered, democratic way. If there were any doubt that the parties had lost their strictly private status, this melding of public and party office into one election process completely removed it.

*Compelling State Interest*
Close to a century has passed since New York and other American states began to transform the major political parties into the semi-public institutions they are today. Non-official parties in New York, such as the Socialist and Socialist Labor parties, can and do organize themselves and select their candidates in any manner they choose, but not political parties whose candidates stand a good chance of being successful. For such parties, the Federal courts have recognized that there is a "compelling state interest" for the state to regulate them, to encourage them—by giving them access to the ballot—and to protect them—by requiring a closed primary. The reason was clearly stated by a Federal district court in 1972 when New York's election law was challenged. Speaking of the role played by political parties in a modern democracy, the court observed that "The entire political process depends largely upon the satisfactory operation of these institutions."[2]

## Political Parties as Organizations

At least on paper all of New York's official political parties can boast of a pyramidal organizational structure which follows the specifications found in the state election law. At the bottom are the many thousand committeepersons, elected from each election district, who when assembled constitute the respective county committees. At the middle level are the respective county chairmen, elected by the county committees. Autonomous in their own jurisdictions and individually wielding great power over nominations and patronage, the 62 county chairmen have provided the core component of party organizational strength in New York, giving the state a decentralized party system.[3] In popular parlance, the county leaders are the "bosses," the most legendary of whom over the past century (e.g., Tweed, Plunkitt, Murphy, DeSapio) have headed the New York County (Manhattan) Democratic organization, Tammany Hall. Outside New York City the committeepersons may be further organized into town and city components, each with its own elected leader. Finally, at the top of the organizational pyramid there is the state committee, whose members are elected from each of the 150 Assembly districts and who elect a state chairman. The election law allows a party limited freedom to modify these structural components; thus in New York City the rules of some county organizations provide for the additional positions of (Assembly) district leader.

Because the names of the state and county chairmen for each party are listed in the state's official publication, the *Legislative Manual,* and also because these officers are periodically called upon to perform specific tasks as specified in the election law (e.g., candidate designation for statewide office, cross-endorsement agreements), there is little doubt that these persons, or at least most of them, are parts of viable organizations. Beyond these top-level officers, however, it is difficult to generalize about party organizational strength in New York. There is no published record of county committeepersons—although their names are on file at the respective county boards of election—and even if such a record were readily available, it would be difficult to interpret. In counties where a party is in the minority, committee posts may be occupied in name only, with the occupant seldom or never participating in party affairs. (Indeed, sometimes he or she can be shown to have moved away or died long ago.) At the opposite extreme, where a party is dominant in the area, committee posts may be highly valued because of the patronage which is associated with them, and, therefore, all are likely to be filled by active party workers. The term "machine" will probably be used by critics to describe such a fully manned and active organizational network.

There are several measures which can be used to help show the presence or absence of an effective county (or town or city) party organization. Most of these point to the same two conclusions: one is that party organizational strength has declined from what it once was; the other is that party organizational strength today varies considerably from one area of the state to another.

One good measure of an effective party organization is its ability to control nominations for public office and ward off primary election challenges. As will be shown in the next chapter, over the years the local political party organizations throughout the state have been very successful in controlling the nomination process. Largely as a result, and also because until 1967 nominations for statewide office were made by party conventions, the parties in New York have long enjoyed the reputation of having organizations which rank among the strongest in the nation. Since 1960, nevertheless, this index of organization strength has shown a marked change; primary elections have become much more frequent than before.

A second measure of party strength is the frequency of competition for the position of party committeeperson. Where these posts are highly valued and where there is factionalism within the ranks, spirited contests for party committee posts may provide the major excitement on primary election day. Certainly such was the case fifty years ago. In 1932, for example, a study of 18 upstate cities found that one-third of the committee posts were contested that year.[4] In 1934 in New York City there were fights for Democratic district leadership posts in all but a few of the City's Assembly districts. Again in the 1950s New York City's primary elections were highlighted by district leadership contests between the "regular" and the "reform" factions of the Democratic party. Such examples of vigorous competition for party positions are less frequent today, and the change seems clearly to reflect the declining role and significance of party activists. The decline in New York City, once home of the strongest county organizations, has been especially dramatic. Today spirited contests for party posts, if occurring at all, are much more likely to be found in the surrounding suburbs than in the City.[5]

The most important job of local party organizations is to "get out the vote" on election day. Accordingly, a third measure of the presence of an effective party organization is high voter turnout and highly partisan voting, even though these aspects of voting behavior are effected by factors other than organizational stimulus. As will be shown in chapter four, over the period 1952–1980 voter turnout in the state declined nearly twenty percentage points. The decline in New York City was especially steep, seeming to confirm that it was here where the decline of "machine politics" was most dramatic. In contrast, in the two counties known for having the two strongest machines in the state, Albany (Democrat) and Nassau (Republican), voter turnout remained high by comparison with the remainder of the state. Thus, in 1970 and 1980 (census years for which accurate voting-age population is available), voter turnout in Nassau was 63 percent and 62 percent, and in Albany 68 percent and 67 percent, compared to a 56 percent and 58 percent rate in the remainder of the state outside New York City.

**Table I.** Voter Independence as Reflected in Percentage of Blank Ballots for State Supreme Court Justice, Gubernatorial Election Years, 1950–1978

|                  | 1950 | 1954 | 1958 | 1962 | 1966 | 1970 | 1974 | 1978 |
|------------------|------|------|------|------|------|------|------|------|
| New York City    | 14.6 | 8.2  | 7.0  | 10.2 | 20.1 | 25.3 | 27.7 | 28.4 |
| Outside the City | 8.6  | 6.6  | 7.0  | 8.3  | 9.0  | 12.3 | 14.1 | 14.8 |
| Nassau County    | 4.2  | 2.8  | 5.5  | 8.1  | 8.0  | 12.1 | 12.5 | 12.1 |
| Albany County    | 3.3  | 2.1  | 2.4  | 3.6  | 6.3  | 10.5 | 11.5 | 11.8 |

Note: When there was no election in a Supreme Court district for the year shown, results for the nearest election year are used.

Probably the best measure of partisan voting on election day is the proportion of voters who choose to participate in the various state Supreme Court contests which appear each year or so at the beginning of the ballot in the state's eleven judicial districts. Because these contests are often meaningless due to Democratic-Republican cross-endorsements, or are unintelligible due to the fact that the canon of judicial ethics prevents candidates from campaigning, the temptation for many voters is to skip past this part of the ballot; only the loyal partisans can be completely depended upon to pull systematically all the levers on the party's row (or column) of the voting machine. Since 1960 such loyalty has shown a dramatic drop. Table I shows the percentage of blank ballots cast for the state Supreme Court posts for the eight gubernatorial election years over the period 1950–1978. Separate totals are shown for New York City, the remainder of the state outside the City, plus Albany and Nassau Counties. It will be seen that the drop in straight-ticket voting was most dramatic in New York City, while the drop in Albany and Nassau was much less than elsewhere.

A final measure of the presence of an effective party organization is the extent to which there is an overlap between party committee personnel and persons on the public payroll. The 1932 study, cited above, found that 19 percent of the committeepersons in the 18 upstate cities held government jobs. For cities noted for their especially strong party organizations, such as Albany (Democrat) and Syracuse (Republican), the percentages were much higher. A 1952 study by the state crime commission reported that in New York City some 90 percent of the district leaders (of both the major parties) were on the public payroll or had been so in the past.[6] Unfortunately there are no recent systematic studies of the overlap in personnel between party committee posts and government employment. However, contemporary journalistic exposés of patronage practices in areas such as Albany and Nassau and Suffolk Counties on Long Island leave little doubt that the nourishment for local organizations is provided by jobs, fees, contracts, and influence-wielding appointments (e.g., zoning boards) given to those who hold committee posts. Almost by definition, strong organization implies the extensive use of these patronage practices; where a local organization is weak, the major cause is usually that, being the minority party in local government, the party has been deprived of such nourishment. Similarly, that the major party organizations remain strong at the level of county chairman is in no small part related to the fact that many of these persons benefit from some kind of patronage, such as "consultantships" in the state legislature. As of 1982 the legislature employed some 3,000 full-time or part-time aides at an annual cost in salaries of $37 million.

## Parties within the Electorate

*Party Enrollment*
New York's political parties are more than legally recognized institutions and more than organizations of activists. Perhaps most important, the parties exist in the enduring loyalties and behavior of defined segments of the electorate.

The most readily available measure of the electorate's commitment to the political parties is to be found in the enrollment figures maintained by the county boards of elections. Ever since the introduction of the state's closed primary system in 1898 these figures have provided a convenient guide to the partisan disposition of New York voters. Table II presents these figures for the first presidential election year (when voter registration is highest) for each decade beginning in 1932.

What is most impressive about enrollment data is their consistency over time. Since 1931 statewide Democratic enrollment has nearly always exceeded Republican enrollment; the major exceptions occurred during the early 1950s. In addition, the two parties' enrollment strength has always paralleled the dichotomy of New York City versus outside the City, with Democrats always being in the large majority in the City and Republicans always being in the large majority in all but a few (five as of 1980) of the state's remaining 57 counties. These consistent patterns leave no doubt that party loyalties are not random, but rather are transmitted from one generation to the next and are strongly affected by a voter's social environment.

Despite the relative stability of party enrollments, three trends have been noticeable. The first has been the decline of Republicanism. Since the 1950s the Republican enrollment proportion has steadily declined while the Democratic proportion has increased. Thus, the statewide Democratic lead of about five percentage points in 1960 increased to over 13 points by 1980. Only a small part of the decline could be accounted for by the inauguration of Conservative party enrollment in 1963. The second discernible trend has been the increase in the number of so-called "independents," i.e., registered voters who have chosen not to enroll in any political party. Between 1960 and 1980 the proportion of such voters more than doubled. Reflecting the first two trends, a third change has been the elimination of the bipolarity which once existed between the parties' enrollment strengths, respectively, in New York City and the remainder of the state. Though the City has remained staunchly Democratic, outside the City has become much more evenly balanced between the two major parties. For example, in 1950 enrollment in the three most populous upstate cities of Buffalo, Rochester, and Syracuse showed a Republican edge over the Democrats of 4, 43, and 42 percentage points, respectively. Thirty years later Democrats outnumbered Republicans in Buffalo and Rochester by 49 and 12 percentage points, respectively, and the Republican edge in Syracuse had been reduced to 10 points. The decline of Republican strength in these upstate cities is especially worthy of note since at one time analysis of New York state politics stressed the fact that these cities, unlike cities in the rest of America, tended to be strongly Republican in preference.[7] The suburbs around New York City have likewise become more evenly balanced; a Republican enrollment edge of 52 percentage points in 1950 had shrunk to 13 points by 1980.

Because of their availability, the party enrollment figures are the data most often cited by journalists as the index of the electorate's partisanship. There is strong evidence, nevertheless, that these figures provide only rough approximations of what they are said to measure. Several analysts have noted that there is a systematic tendency for many voters to enroll in the party which is dominant in the area where they live, regardless of their own partisan preference.[8] The tendency can be seen reflected in the fact that invariably the dominant party in an area will perform less well on election day than its enrollment figures would suggest it should, while the reverse is true in those areas where the party enrollment is low. For example, in 1978 Hugh Carey, on the Democratic line of the ballot, polled only 58 percent of the New York City vote, in contrast to the 72 percent Democratic enrollment in the City. Yet in Nassau County, Democrat Carey polled fully 43 percent of the vote, despite Democratic enrollment there being only 34 percent.

Other evidence suggests that over the years the enrollment figures may also have overstated the number of partisans and understated the number of independents. Until 1976 there was no obvious way for independents to record their feelings. When registering with the local board of election, the new voter would be presented with a form which contained the names of all the official parties, with instructions to check the box next to the party of his or her choice. There were no instructions for the person who did not wish to enroll in any party; the registrant was not told that he or she had the option of leaving all the boxes blank. In 1976, however, mail registration was introduced, and the new form which was designed for mail registrants carried an additional box, one marked with the notation "I do not wish to enroll in any political party." Immediately the proportion of independents increased. To confirm the cause-and-effect relationship, an election commissioner in Monroe County compared the choices made in 1976 by the mail

**Table II.** Three indices of Political Party Preferences

## I. Percent of all Enrolled Voters

|      | State | | | New York City | | | Outside N.Y. City | | |
|------|-------|------|-------|------|------|-------|------|------|-------|
|      | *Dem.* | *Rep.* | *Other* | *Dem.* | *Rep.* | *Other* | *Dem.* | *Rep.* | *Other* |
| *1932* | 53.8 | 44.9 | 1.3 | 77.2 | 21.0 | 1.8 | 32.4 | 66.6 | 0.9 |
| *1940* | 53.1 | 44.1 | 2.8 | 71.4 | 23.8 | 4.7 | 32.5 | 66.9 | 0.6 |
| *1952* | 47.2 | 50.4 | 2.4 | 65.9 | 29.7 | 4.4 | 29.4 | 70.2 | 0.5 |
| *1960* | 51.9 | 46.7 | 1.4 | 72.2 | 25.6 | 2.2 | 35.0 | 64.3 | 0.6 |
| *1972* | 54.6 | 41.4 | 4.0 | 75.1 | 20.0 | 5.0 | 39.9 | 56.8 | 3.3 |
| *1980* | 56.5 | 40.4 | 3.1 | 81.0 | 16.1 | 2.9 | 44.2 | 54.4 | 3.3 |

II. Enrolled as Percent of all Registered Voters [a]

| | Dem. | Rep. | Other | Blank | Dem. | Rep. | Other | Blank | Dem. | Rep. | Other | Blank |
|---|---|---|---|---|---|---|---|---|---|---|---|---|
| 1960 | 47.8 | 43.1 | 1.3 | 7.9 | 67.6 | 23.9 | 2.1 | 6.3 | 31.8 | 58.5 | 0.6 | 9.1 |
| 1972 | 48.7 | 36.8 | 3.5 | 11.0 | 68.2 | 18.1 | 4.5 | 9.2 | 35.0 | 49.9 | 2.9 | 12.2 |
| 1980 | 47.0 | 33.5 | 2.6 | 16.9 | 70.1 | 13.9 | 2.5 | 13.5 | 34.4 | 44.2 | 2.7 | 18.8 |

III. Vote for State Supreme Court Justice

| | Dem. | Rep. | Other | Blank | Dem. | Rep. | Other | Blank | Dem. | Rep. | Other | Blank |
|---|---|---|---|---|---|---|---|---|---|---|---|---|
| 1958 | 42.6 | 44.7 | 5.7 | 7.0 | 49.1 | 35.0 | 8.9 | 7.0 | 35.9 | 54.6 | 2.5 | 7.0 |
| 1962 | 41.3 | 46.0 | 3.8 | 8.9 | 49.8 | 31.8 | 8.1 | 10.2 | 37.6 | 52.2 | 1.9 | 8.3 |
| 1966 | 39.6 | 30.4 | 13.3 | 16.7 | 42.0 | 22.6 | 15.3 | 20.1 | 34.0 | 48.0 | 9.0 | 9.0 |
| 1970 | 36.7 | 30.9 | 13.3 | 19.1 | 40.5 | 18.5 | 15.7 | 25.3 | 32.4 | 44.5 | 10.8 | 12.3 |
| 1978 | 41.2 | 28.7 | 8.6 | 21.5 | 46.2 | 16.1 | 9.3 | 28.4 | 36.3 | 40.8 | 8.1 | 14.8 |
| 1980 | 38.3 | 33.2 | 6.1 | 22.4 | 43.7 | 18.1 | 7.5 | 30.7 | 34.8 | 43.3 | 5.0 | 16.9 |

[a] Statewide data on non-enrolled voters not available for earlier years.

Note: When a judicial district did not hold an election in the year shown, the nearest surrounding year is used.

registrants with the choices made by those who came in person to the election board and, thus, who used the old form. The results were conclusive: among the mail registrants 36 percent chose the "not to enroll" option whereas among the in-person registrants the proportion leaving all the boxes blank was only 11 percent.

*Other Evidence*

Because enrollment figures provide only a rough guide to basic party preferences, it is wise to look at two other available measures. One of these is party identification as revealed by opinion surveys. Such evidence is fragmentary and available only for recent years. Nevertheless, it does confirm the basic pattern of party division which is suggested by the enrollment figures. A 1980 survey, for example, found 44 percent of the New York electorate to be self-described Democrats and 37 percent to be self-described Republicans.[9]

There is another measure of party preference, however, one which is more readily available than opinion surveys and which is based on actual voting behavior. As suggested in the previous section, this is the pattern of partisan preferences which is recorded in races for the post of state Supreme Court justice in the eleven judicial districts. Cross-endorsements or, where there is a contest among candidates, the absence of campaigning result in the pattern of recorded preferences (including blank ballots) being the pattern of partisan preferences, even though these may be influenced by the major contests of the particular election. The bottom of Table II presents these measurements for six typical gubernatorial or (1980) presidential election years (years of extreme political volatility—1964, 1972, 1974—have been avoided). These data confirm the geographical and longitudinal patterns shown by enrollment figures. Even more than those figures, they emphasize the steep decline of Republicanism during the decade of the 1960s. By this measurement, Republicans outnumbered Democrats in the state by about five percentage points through the election of 1962; but by 1966 their numbers had dropped by about 15 percentage points—despite the fact that in that year the Republican candidate for governor was victorious. The party never recovered from that decline, which began two years previously when Goldwater headed the ticket. It was not, however, the Democrats who benefited since their proportion of support also slipped. Rather, it was the independent voter, refusing to participate in these judicial contests, who became more conspicuous, amounting to over 22 percent of the electorate by 1980.

### Party as Cue

The electorate's basic partisan loyalties, to the extent they exist, mark the starting point for each electoral contest; they are the latent attitudes which set the odds before candidates are chosen or issues are raised. The evidence which has been presented shows that over the past several decades these odds have moved in favor of the Democrats. The fundamental question, however, is whether or not voters, when casting ballots for the all-important executive and legislative offices of government, do in fact vote for their party, or at least vote for *a* party, rather than choose according to other factors such as the personal qualities of the candidates or the issues. Although survey responses from individual voters provide the most satisfactory data for answering that question, election results provide useful clues.

Before examining the biennial election results in New York, it is instructive to look at New York's village and school board elections, where the ballot shows only the names of the candidates running for the various offices. The state legislation governing these contests obviously envisages elections without parties, and, true to this intent, the local branches of the official political parties usually do not participate. In fact, however, what often happens is that the various candidates will organize themselves into "teams" or "parties," carrying attractive labels such as "low tax" or "citizens," and the voters will respond to this guidance by awarding to each member of the respective groups approximately the same number of votes. Even at this small-community level, therefore, parties apparently are needed to structure the electoral choice.

Primary elections provide additional evidence for the conclusion that where there are no parties they have to be invented. When an insurgent faction challenges the entire slate of organization-backed candidates, all the insurgents and all the organization candidates will usually campaign as defined groups, urging voters to support their slate. Voters, in turn, will usually respond by voting straight "reform" or straight "organization," despite the difficulty of doing so in the absence of ballot identification. (Election boards have refused requests that the respective sides in primary battles be grouped together on the ballot).

Good government groups in New York and elsewhere have usually been critical of this tendency of voters to vote the "straight ticket." Accordingly, in 1913 their pressure resulted in New York changing its paper ballot format for the November elections from the party column with the circle at the top for straight party voting, to the so-called office-block ballot where candidates are grouped together according to the office for which they are running. Today New York is thus classified by the Council of State Government's *Book of the States* as one of the 29 states which does not permit straight-ticket voting with a single mark or single voting-machine lever, and the term "office block" is still applied to the state. That term is very misleading, however. Since voting machines became compulsory for general elections in 1938, New York in fact has had a ballot format which makes straight-party voting very easy because all of a party's candidates are listed on a single horizontal row on the machine or (as in New York City) in a single vertical column. The slogan often heard at election time, "Vote Row *A* All the Way," accurately indicates how similar today's ballot is to the pre-1913 paper ballot.

The aggregate vote at New York's biennial elections suggests that most voters do in fact vote straight party, or nearly so, even though (as indicated above) many may skip over judicial and other offices of low visibility. One study, covering the period 1932–1970, and based on comparison of the party vote for president, governor, U. S. senator, and the cumulative, statewide congressional vote, ranked New York among the highest states in the nation in the degree of straight-ticket voting.[10] Table III presents similar comparisons. As will be seen, all of the totals for executive and the three legislative offices are usually strikingly similar. Where wide discrepancies occur, they have been with respect to the presidential or gubernatorial totals compared with the three legislative totals. Thus in 1964 there was a twelve-percentage-point difference in the heavy Democratic presidential vote (Johnson) and the three Democratic legislative totals, which were much lower. Wide differences between the Republican gubernatorial vote under Rockefeller (1962, 1966, 1970) and the Republican vote for the three sets of legislative offices are also apparent. These differences, and the frequently wide year-to-year differences for the executive vote, suggest that party voting for these offices of high visibility is much less than it is at the legislative level where all totals are similar, where year-to-year changes are small, and where, to the extent changes occur, they usually affect all three legislative totals in the same direction.

Despite the gaps which often appear between the top-of-the-ticket vote and a party's legislative vote, all four of the totals sometimes rise and fall in tandem. The ability of the national party to pull down to defeat its state counterpart was dramatically illustrated in both 1964 and 1974 when first an unpopular presidential candidate (Goldwater) and then a scandal-ridden Republican presidency (Watergate) resulted in drops of about nine and six percentage points, respectively, for the three Republican legislative totals. Yet the record also shows that there are limits on the ability of a popular or unpopular candidate at the top of the ticket to affect the vote cast for legislators. The McGovern candidacy in 1972 did not noticeably hurt Democratic legislative candidates that year, and neither the 1976 Carter victory nor the 1980 Reagan victory seem to have had a positive impact on these candidates' party colleagues.

If there is one trend which is discernible from the figures in Table III, it is that party voting appears to be decreasing, as might be expected in light of the other evidence pointing to increasing voter independence. The vote for the state Senate became especially autonomous in the 1970s, accounting for the fact that this body remained in Republican control while the Assembly and congressional delegations had majority representation of Democrats.

One additional type of evidence for the conclusion that the overwhelming majority of voters appear to be guided by the party cue is provided when a candidate runs for office first with one party label and later with another. James Buckley ran for the U. S. Senate in 1968 as the Conservative party candidate (and without the informal Republican backing he had two years later) and polled only 17 percent of the vote; in 1976, running now as both the Conservative and the Republican nominee, Buckley polled 45 percent of the vote. Jacob Javits polled 45 percent of the vote in 1974 running as a Republican and a Liberal; but in 1980, deprived of the Republican nomination and running only as a Liberal, he polled only 11 percent of the vote. In 1975 a candidate for the Suffolk

**Table III.** Party Voting in New York, 1960–1980

| | Democratic Percentage of Total Statewide Vote* | | | | | | | | | | |
|---|---|---|---|---|---|---|---|---|---|---|---|
| | *1960* | *1962* | *1964* | *1966* | *1968* | *1970* | *1972* | *1974* | *1976* | *1978* | *1980* |
| Pres./Gov. | 46.4 | 43.1 | 62.5 | 37.3 | 44.1 | 39.4 | 37.8 | 54.6 | 48.7 | 49.3 | 42.9 |
| Congress | 45.6 | 44.1 | 50.8 | 41.3 | 40.3 | 39.4 | 41.6 | 46.4 | 48.6 | 44.6 | 40.8 |
| State Sen. | 44.9 | 42.8 | 49.5 | 38.4 | 34.0 | 35.4 | 37.4 | 41.4 | 39.6 | 38.2 | 35.3 |
| State Assem. | 45.4 | 43.4 | 49.5 | 39.6 | 37.6 | 36.2 | 39.8 | 44.4 | 45.6 | 42.4 | 40.0 |

| | Republican Percentage of Total Statewide Vote* | | | | | | | | | | |
|---|---|---|---|---|---|---|---|---|---|---|---|
| Pres./Gov. | 46.7 | 52.0 | 30.7 | 43.7 | 43.2 | 51.2 | 52.2 | 40.0 | 42.4 | 43.7 | 45.5 |
| Congress | 44.2 | 45.4 | 36.9 | 38.6 | 37.4 | 36.0 | 39.9 | 33.3 | 34.4 | 36.4 | 38.7 |
| State Sen. | 44.4 | 45.7 | 36.3 | 39.2 | 40.1 | 38.0 | 41.3 | 36.0 | 38.7 | 41.1 | 40.1 |
| State Assem. | 44.1 | 45.4 | 36.5 | 38.0 | 38.4 | 36.9 | 40.5 | 34.9 | 35.5 | 38.3 | 37.5 |

* including blank ballots

Note: The percentages in the table refer to a party's vote as recorded on the party's line on the voting machine. A party's candidate often polls more votes as a result of being cross-endorsed by a minor party.

County Legislature, running as an independent, polled 14 percent of the vote; two years later, running against the same candidate and in the same district, but this time as the Republican and Conservative nominee, the candidate polled 54 percent of the vote. These examples clearly illustrate that the often-heard claim "I vote for the person, not the party" does not accurately portray the behavior of the bulk of the electorate.

## Parties as Cohesive Groups of Legislators

Accounts of the legislative process in New York have stressed the very strong role played by political parties. When in the majority, a party's legislators will unite to control all of the positions of power, such as the Assembly speakership and committee chairmanships, and whether in the majority or minority, a party's legislators will vote as a relatively cohesive bloc on major policy questions, such as budgetary and other proposals which emanate from the governor's office. A study done in the 1960s ranked New York as having among the most cohesive legislative parties of any in the nation, and certainly more cohesive than the congressional parties at the national level. A related finding was that only Rhode Island and Pennsylvania exceeded New York in the proportion of controversial legislative matters which were decided by a party vote, defined as a vote in which the majority of one legislative party votes one way and the majority of the other legislative party votes the other.[11]

*Parties as Natural Communities*

Part of the reason for the highly partisan behavior in the legislature has already been suggested: the electoral fortunes of legislative party members are interdependent. Another reason is the structure of rewards and punishments which the legislative party leaders control (e.g., committee assignments, facilitation of passage of sponsored bills, campaign assistance). It would be wrong, however, to think of the New York legislative parties as bound together by nothing more than the enlightened self-interest of their members. At least as important is the fact that the legislative parties form natural communities.

Reflecting the geographical pattern of electoral support, most Democrats in the two legislative houses have come from New York City whereas most Republicans have come from areas outside the City. In 1980, for example, two-thirds of the Democratic Assembly members represented City districts, and some 90 percent of the Republican Assembly members represented districts outside the City. Since the interests of New York City have always posed major policy questions facing the legislature each year—especially finance-related questions, such as aid formulas—the dominant City voice within the Democratic legislative parties and the relative absence of that voice within the Republican legislative parties have inevitably made those parties the spokesmen for divergent interests.

In addition to being spokesmen for the needs and interests of their districts, legislators may be expected to mirror the broad attitudes of their constitutents. On this dimension, too, the Republican and Democratic legislative parties form distinguishable communities. Historically the major attitudinal dimension dividing the New York electorate has been that of pro- and anti-New York City, an antagonism rooted as much in sociological as in political differences. It is this factor which accounted for upstate New York being dominantly Republican for many years. The fact that these upstate areas have now become decreasingly Republican thus suggests that this attitudinal bipolarity has significantly decreased. Nevertheless, other evidence shows the persistence of sharp differences between the policy attitudes of voters in New York City and voters elsewhere. The periodic results of statewide referenda are instructive. When asked to approve bond issues or when asked to approve constitutional amendments relating to indebtedness, a majority of City voters casting ballots on these questions will almost invariably vote yes while outside the City the majority of participants will almost invariably vote no. In popular terminology, City voters are most likely to take the "liberal" position, favoring government action to solve problems, while non-City voters are likely to take the opposite, "conservative" position. In 1975 a proposed equal rights amendment to the state constitution produced a similar liberal-conservative split: 59 percent of the City participants voted yes, compared to only 38 percent of the outside-the-City participants who did so.

Despite the factors which bind together the members of the respective legislative parties, both parties have become more heterogeneous as the result of (1) the growth of the suburbs around New York City to form a distinctive set of area-based interests and attitudes; (2) the court-ordered reapportionment of the 1960s which allowed this growth to find political expression; and (3) the increasing ability of Democrats to win in areas outside New York City. The Democratic party in the Assembly has become an especially difficult mixture, being composed by 1980 of approximately two-thirds City, 22 percent upstate, and 12 percent suburbs. For the Republicans the proportions were about 60 percent upstate, 30 percent suburbs, and 10 percent City. Referenda results illustrate the challenge to the parties' cohesion: almost invariably the suburbs occupy a position midway between the conservatism of upstate and the liberalism of the City. Thus the City, suburban, and upstate "yes" percentages for the 1975 ERA referendum were 59 percent, 45 percent, and 35 percent.

*Roll Call Analysis*
One convenient way to observe the contrasting outlooks of the Democratic and Republican legislative parties and the degree of their cohesion is to examine the roll call votes recorded by legislators on those issues on which each legislator is free to vote his or her own mind, unhindered by the demands of leaders for party loyalty. Each year the New York Civil Liberties Union tracks a selec-

tion of these votes and then issues a rating score for each legislator, a 100 percent score signifying perfect agreement with the NYCLU's position and a zero score signifying complete disagreement. Usually there are a dozen or so votes included in the annual index, relating to issues such as the death penalty, abortion, rights of defendants, prison reform, school integration, drug laws, women's rights, and electoral reform. These are issues on which there is usually said to be a "liberal" and a "conservative" position.

Table IV shows the average NYCLU score for all Democratic and Republican Assembly members for the annual legislative sessions 1972–1980. The difference between the two parties is clear; each year that difference was about 30 percentage points. Party affiliation is thus obviously a very important factor in explaining policy views. Having said that much, we must nevertheless realize that the figures shown in the table are averages; some legislators

**Table IV.** NYCLU Ratings of Democratic and Republican Assembly Members 1972–1980

| | I. Average NYCLU Ratings | | | | | | | | |
| | *1972* | *1973* | *1974* | *1975* | *1976* | *1977* | *1978* | *1979* | *1980* |
|---|---|---|---|---|---|---|---|---|---|
| Democratic | 55.2 | 77.5 | 62.9 | NA | 69.3 | 66.9 | 63.9 | 78.4 | 68.0 |
| Republican | 27.7 | 30.1 | 27.6 | NA | 28.5 | 37.7 | 25.1 | 39.8 | 30.6 |

| | II. Intra-Party Variation[a] in NYCLU Ratings | | | | | | | | |
| | *1972* | *1973* | *1974* | *1975* | *1976* | *1977* | *1978* | *1979* | *1980* |
|---|---|---|---|---|---|---|---|---|---|
| Democratic | 67.6 | 62.7 | 58.8 | NA | 51.2 | 52.3 | 60.9 | 60.0 | 50.0 |
| Republican | 14.1 | 7.4 | 14.8 | NA | 36.7 | 8.3 | 24.6 | 19.0 | 32.4 |

III. Average NYCLU Ratings for Districts Changing Party, and for Districts Changing Members only

| | *1974 Election* | | *1976 Election* | | *1978 Election* | |
|---|---|---|---|---|---|---|
| | *Pre* | *Post* | *Pre* | *Post* | *Pre* | *Post* |
| Districts Changing Parties | | | | | | |
| Rep. to Dem. | 27.2 | 52.8 | 40.0 | 62.7 | 27.3 | 47.5 |
| Dem. to Rep. | 80.0 | 21.0 | 58.8 | 37.7 | 51.3 | 34.0 |
| Districts Changing Members Only | | | | | | |
| Remain Dem. | 70.5 | 81.9 | 65.8 | 66.4 | 66.4 | 82.1 |
| Remain Rep. | 34.4 | 26.6 | 45.6 | 32.8 | 30.8 | 35.4 |

[a] Percent of scores 15 points or more above or below the party average.

fall below the average for their party and some score well above the average. As the middle part of the table makes clear, the Democratic party has been especially torn by a variety of outlooks within its ranks; many of its elected members consistently score in the 80–100 range on the NYCLU index while some are to be found in the 20–40 range. As can be seen, in every year shown in the table at least half of the Democratic Assembly members scored 15 points above the party average or 15 points below that average. In contrast, the Republicans have been bound by a much more uniform outlook. There is no neat and ready explanation for the wide deviation within Democratic ranks. Democratic Assembly members from New York City are to be found in more or less equal numbers at the high end of the NYCLU index and at the low end. So are Democrats from the suburbs, and so are Democrats from highly competitive districts and those from completely safe districts. The only variable which seems to be related systematically with the NYCLU scores is the pattern of cross-endorsement, a topic to be discussed in chapter three.

One interpretation of the difference, on average, between the policy views of Republican and Democratic legislators is that the legislators are expressing the views of their districts. Another interpretation is that the parties are attracting, nominating, and electing to their respective ranks persons of contrasting outlooks. To show which interpretation is more warranted the bottom of Table IV presents an analysis of NYCLU scores for those legislators who were not re-elected in the election following the recorded roll call votes, being replaced by a representative of the opposing party. If the nature of the constituency is the controlling factor in determining a legislator's policy position, then the NYCLU score for a legislator's replacement should be relatively the same as that previously recorded by the district's representative. As will be seen from the table, such is not the case. Among the districts changing from Republican to Democrat, for each period shown there was a large average jump on the NYCLU index, while among districts changing from Democrat to Republican there was a large average change in the opposite direction. Obviously party is independently related to a legislator's policy orientation. That conclusion is reinforced when we look at those districts whose representative did not run for re-election and was replaced by another of the same party. Only small changes occurred in the NYCLU scores: Democratic districts remained relatively high on the index and Republican districts remained relatively low.


## New York as a Multi-Party System

As of 1980 there were three minor parties in the state, ones which had acquired official status in 1946, 1962, and 1978, respectively. These were the Liberal, Conservative, and Right to Life parties. New York thus stood out as a glaring exception to the generalization found in American government textbooks that the United States has a two-party system. Of course, there is hardly a state in the union which has not, at some time or other, had one or more minor parties appearing on the ballot.[12] The distinctiveness of New York's multi-party system, therefore, is that it is an institutionalized system. Measures of party institutionalization are permanence, support, official recognition, penetration, and organization.

Looking at the first of these measures, if we examine the round of state gubernatorial elections taking place during the period 1975–1978, we find only three states other than New York where the ballot featured a gubernatorial candidate of a minor party (i.e., a party other than Democratic or Republican) which had acquired a degree of *permanence,* having put up a candidate in as many as three immediately preceding contests. These were Kansas (Prohibition), New Jersey (Socialist Labor), and Washington (Socialist Labor). In New York the record of continuous participation by minor parties extended for eight consecutive gubernatorial elections, back to 1946 when the Liberal party first appeared.

As for the second measure of institutionalization, *support,* if we take the convenient cut-off point of five percent, we see that in none of the three states mentioned did the total party vote reach five percent of the total vote. Indeed, outside New York, from 1950 through 1978 there were only nine instances, scattered across seven states, where the total minor party gubernatorial vote ever reached that threshold. In New York, in contrast, the minor party vote has totaled at least five percent in every gubernatorial election since 1934. Membership is also a measure of party support. Although New York's Liberal and Conservative parties could each, as of 1980, boast of only between one and two percent of the state's registered voters, even that small proportion was high by comparison with the pattern in the other states which maintain such data.

The reason that many states' registration figures do not show minor party membership is, of course, that in those states the minor parties have not met the state's requirement for *official recognition*. In the period 1956–1976 there were only three states outside New York where a minor party had survived long enough to have its candidates chosen in state-run primaries in two or more consecutive election years (California, Pennsylvania, Wisconsin). In contrast, in New York state-run primaries for the Liberal party had occurred since 1947, and for the Conservative party since 1963.

In terms of the scope of *penetration* into the various contests for state and local offices, New York's minor parties are again distinctive. If we look at the readily available data for 1978 congressional elections, we see that outside New York there were only three states in which a minor party contested not only that year's (or the appropriately preceding year's) gubernatorial contest, but also contested as many as two congressional districts. These states were California (8 and 7 districts, respectively for its two minor parties), and Minnesota and New Jersey (3 districts each). In contrast, New York's Liberal and Conservative Parties in 1978 entered candidates in 32 and 35, respectively, of the state's 39 districts. The unavailability of comparative data for state legislative races and local government contests prevents us from making precise comparisons of minor party penetration at these levels of government. It seems reasonable to assume, however, that if the data were available, the pattern would be found to be the same as that for the congressional races. In the New York state legislative elections of 1978, for example, the two minor parties contested 98 and 122 respectively, of the 150 Assembly districts; they contested 41 and 52 of the 60 Senate districts. To cite one contrast, in California's legislative elections of 1978 the two parties which contested the gubernatorial office contested only 13 and 7, respectively, of the 120 legislative seats. In the 1977 local elections in New York the two official minor parties were also well represented. In New York City, the Liberals contested all 14 of the city-wide offices to be filled, and the Conservatives all but three. In the 29 counties which elected county legislatures that year, the Conservatives contested 349 of the 549 seats to be filled; the Liberals contested 73 seats.

The final measure of party institutionalization, the reality and complexity of party *organization,* is the most difficult one to analyze with any precision, for reasons already mentioned. There seems little doubt that outside New York City the Liberal party can boast of hardly any organizational strength at all, and in the 1960s the election law was amended to acknowledge that reality. Conservative party organization within New York City is similarly weak. Yet all three minor parties can boast of some organizational activists in areas where they enjoy electoral support. Nourishing the organizational vitality of the minor parties has been the patronage doled out to them by the major parties (see chapter three), as well as the ideological commitment which is suggested by their labels. (By 1980, only Right to Life activists were known for their greater concern with the latter over for former.)

## New York as a Competitive Party System

New York State has always been ranked by political scientists as having a competitive party system. Exactly how New York has compared with other states, however, has depended on the measurement used. In one study, covering the period 1956–1970, New York was ranked among the *least* competitive of the 28 states which were judged to have a competitive party system. New York came close to being ranked as dominantly Republican.[13] Yet another study, covering the period 1932–1970, ranked New York tied with Indiana as the *most* competitive state in the nation.[14] The first study used as one of several measures of competitiveness the number of offices won, and thus was heavily influenced by the fact that the Republicans controlled the governorship and both houses of the state legislature during most of the period covered. The second study not only embraced a longer time span but used as the one measure of competitiveness the margin of votes separating the winner and the runner-up for selected statewide offices.

By the measure of the number of offices won, during the 1970s and early 1980s New York definitely veered away from its tilt toward being dominated by the Republican party. As of the end of 1982, Democrats had won the last three gubernatorial contests, had won control of the Assembly in five consecutive elections, in 1976 and 1982 had elected a U. S. senator, and in 1976 had carried the state for the party's presidential candidate. This record of success was balanced by the Republicans having elected a governor (1970), a U. S. senator (1980), two presidential candidates (1972, 1980), and having retained their long-standing control of the state Senate. Perhaps the best reflection of the state's competitiveness was provided by the electoral record for two other statewide offices: in every quadrennial election from 1954 through 1982 voters had elected a state comptroller of one party and a state attorney general of the opposite party—a vivid example not only of competitiveness but also of split-ticket voting.

By the second measure of party competitiveness—the margin separating the winning and runner-up candidate—New York also remained highly competitive during the 1970s and early 1980s. Despite a few one-sided outcomes, during the 1970–1982 period half of the twelve contests for president, governor, and U. S. senator were decided by margins of less than six percentage points.

That by the 1980s the New York party system had become increasingly competitive could be attributed in part to increased voter independence, in part to the court-ordered reapportionment of the 1960s, and in part to the increasing role played by the minor parties. Reflecting the last-mentioned factor, in four of the five U.S. senatorial elections held from 1968 to 1980 the winning candidate received less than 50 percent of the vote because of the votes polled by a minor party candidate. (The gubernatorial elections of 1954 and 1966 also featured minority outcomes.) Even more important for political competitiveness was the ability of the minor parties, through the cross-endorsement system, to provide the balance of power between the two major parties. This aspect of competitiveness will be discussed in chapter three.

Although New York continues to be highly competitive at the statewide level, it is equally true that most areas of the state are better described as being areas of one-party dominance. Probably the best known example of one-party domination of local government is New York City. There Republican candidates for city-wide office have never had any chance of being elected on their own; they always have had to rely on help from minor parties. Even the city council districts have been dominated by Democrats. In an attempt to correct one-party domination of the council, the City resorted to proportional representation during the decade 1937–1947 and in 1962 turned to today's device of including in the council two members elected at large from each of the five boroughs. Under the rules, a party may nominate only one candidate for these two slots. (In 1982 the system was challenged as unconstitutional.)

Outside New York City, in the 57 county governments and 931 town governments, the situation is the reverse. Here it is the Republican party which is usually dominant. As of 1980, 9 of the 14 county executives were Republican, as were the large majority of town supervisors. In addition to the fact that Republican voters have usually outnumbered Democratic voters in these jurisdictions, at-large election systems for the town councils and for the county legislatures have prevented pockets of Democratic strength from being represented. All but a few of the towns operate under at-large systems for their legislative bodies, as do over half of the counties.

At the congressional and state legislative levels, too, non-competitiveness is the norm. At any given election all but a few of the districts will be won by the same party which carried them before. Thus, in the four elections held from 1974 through 1980 the number of the 150 Assembly seats changing party control was 21, 11, 9, and 9, respectively. In addition, the margins by which legislative districts are won are usually very wide; well over two-thirds are won by margins of 20 percentage points or more. (The aggregate legislative statistics shown in Table III can thus be very misleading.) For those who believe in the value of *district* competitiveness—to make the elected representative responsive to district voters, out of fear of defeat—or for those who believe in the value of *statewide* competition—to make the party majority in Albany responsive to the state electorate out of fear of defeat—the New York party system left much to be desired.

## Conclusion

The purpose of this chapter has been to analyze the basic components of New York's political parties and party system. Invariably frequent reference has been made to primary elections, the cross-endorsement system, voter participation, legislative apportionment, and systems of election. The following chapters will examine each of these topics in greater detail.

# Notes

1. Thus a *designation* petition (see chapter 2) for Congress, state Senate and Assembly requires, respectively 1,250, 1,000 and 500 signatures, whereas an independent *nomination* petition requires 3,500, 3,000 and 1,500 signatures.

2. *Rosario* v. *Rockefeller,* 458 F. 2d 649 (1972), p. 652.

3. In many other states party organization is more centralized. See Robert J. Huckshorn, *Party Leadership in the States,* University of Massachusetts Press (Amherst, 1976), pp. 234–39.

4. William E. Mosher, "Party and Government Control at the Grass Roots," *National Municipal Review,* Vol. 24 (1935), p. 15 ff.

5. In towns located in counties too small to be subject to party nominations through the primary system (population less than 750,000) and thus where nominations may be made by a party committee, a committee-post contest may be a surrogate for the direct primary.

6. Wallace S. Sayre and Herbert Kaufman, *Governing New York City,* Norton (New York, 1965), p. 463; see also the data on party activists and mayoral cabinet appointments on pp. 218–19.

7. The observation was made by Ralph Straetz and Frank Munger, *New York Politics,* New York University Press (New York, 1960), p. 46.

8. The most comprehensive analysis will be found in Gerald Benjamin, "Patterns in New York State Politics," in Robert H. Connery and Gerald Benjamin, eds., *Governing New York State: The Rockefeller Years,* American Academy of Political Science (New York, 1974), pp. 31–44.

9. *New York Times/CBS* survey published in the *Times,* October 21, 1980. See also the survey published in David M. Kovenock, James W. Prothro, and Associates, *Explaining the Vote,* Institute in Social Science (Chapel Hill, 1973).

10. Paul T. David, *Party Strength in the United States,* University Press of Virginia (Charlottesville, 1972), p. 22.

11. Hugh L. LeBlanc, "Voting in State Senates: Party and Constituency Influences," *Midwest Journal of Political Science,* Vol. 13 (February, 1969), p. 36. The best accounts of legislative politics in New York state will be found in Alan G. Hevesi, *Legislative Politics in New York State,* Praeger (New York, 1975), and Leigh Stelzer and James Riedel, *Capitol Goods,* Graduate School of Public Affairs, SUNY Albany (Albany, 1976).

12. By far the most colorful party labels appearing on the ballot are to be found in New Jersey, e.g., "Axe the Tax," "Politicians Are Crooks," "Down with Lawyers," and "Taxpayers Only Friend." These examples serve as useful reminders that ballot names need not denote an institutionalized political party.

13. Austin Ranney, "Parties in State Politics," in Herbert Jacob and Kenneth N. Vines, eds. *Politics in the American States,* Little, Brown (Boston, 1971), p. 87.

14. Paul T. David, p. 50.

# 2.

# Primary Elections in New York State: An Historical Perspective

DEMOCRACY IS often defined as the ability of citizens to choose the officials who govern them. Evidence of this ability is most apparent on election day as citizens choose among the names appearing on the ballot. The names on the ballot, however, have been winnowed from a much wider range of possible candidates. Normally that winnowing is done by the political parties. Some independent candidates, to be sure, may be found on the ballot, but because the voter will usually pay little attention to them, it is the selection by the political parties, i.e., the party *nominations,* which rivals in significance the final selection done by the citizens on election day.

Outside the United States the nominating procedures used by parties are determined by the parties themselves. Normally the procedure calls for the choice of candidate(s) to be made by a relatively small group of party activists at the appropriate level of government, e.g., leading members of the district party branch selecting a candidate to run for the national legislature. In contrast, in New York, as in the other American states, the parties' procedure for candidate nomination is governed by state law. Only when relatively minor offices are to be filled (village offices and offices in most towns) are the parties free to follow their own methods of candidate nomination.[1] For other offices the selection procedures are carefully specified in New York's election law.[2]

Those procedures form the subject of this chapter. They can be discussed conveniently under four major headings: (1) the indirect primary, (2) the direct primary, (3) statewide office and the challenge primary, and (4) today's indirect primaries.

## The Indirect Primary

In his classic study of American political parties published in 1902, Moisel Ostrogorsky used as synonyms the terms "caucuses," "primary assemblies," and "primary elections."[3] Although such usage seems strange today, for the period Ostrogorsky was describing these terms were indeed interchangeable; they referred to *meetings* of party members held for the purpose of electing convention delegates. In the beginning of the Republic candidates for public office were nominated by legislators as they met in the halls of the state or national legislature in their respective party caucuses. With the advent of Jacksonian democracy, however, this method of candidate selection—pejoratively known at the congressional level as "King Caucus"—was abandoned in favor of the seemingly more democratic method of nomination by party convention. What made the new method seem more democratic was the fact that the delegates to these nominating conventions were chosen, directly or indirectly, by the party rank-and-file membership meeting at the district (e.g., election district, legislative district) level. Sometimes, as in the case of a congressional nomination, the subsequent convention would directly select the party's nominee; other times, as in the case of the statewide offices, that convention would merely select delegates to attend a higher-level convention where the nominations would be made. In either case the primary meetings for delegate election were the first step in a two-step, and sometimes three-step, nomination process.

For many years these primary meetings, as well as the subsequent party nominating conventions, remained private affairs, completely unregulated by law. The consequences were vividly described by Ostrogorski and other reform-minded critics in prose heavily laced with tones of moral outrage. The dominant clique of the party—variously called the "machine," the "ring," or simply the "bosses"—were charged by the critics with using every conceivable tactic to control the delegate selection process: scheduling the primary assemblies at inconvenient times and places; giving no public notice of the time and place of the meetings; packing the hall with "gangs" of nonresidents imported for the occasion; running the meeting by voice vote or, if paper ballots were used, stuffing the ballot boxes. In all such accounts New York, and especially New York City and its infamous Tammany Hall Democratic party organization, were prominently featured.

It is perhaps not surprising, then, that New York State was among the first two states (the other was California) to enact (in 1866) legislation designed to curb primary assembly abuses.[4] This initial legislation was limited, however, in both coverage and scope: it applied only to Brooklyn and Buffalo, and the law merely made it a misdemeanor for anyone to bribe or intimidate a primary voter. Later legislation expanded the coverage—New York City was included in 1883—and the scope of activities regulated. In 1887, for example, the law was amended to require the posting of notices of primary meetings and to provide for the appointment by the candidates of poll watchers. However, these and other provisions of the law were filled with loopholes and, hence, did little to still the cries of the critics. The nature of the Tammany primary meetings in 1888 is suggested by the following account:[5]

> In the fourth assembly district, the [newspaper] reporter attended from 7 to 9 P.M.; he saw people sitting about the room playing poker and other games of cards; the meeting was not called to order until 8:40 P.M. because the man with the ballots did not arrive. It was then moved that the secretary be authorized to cast one vote for the society; which being done, the meeting was adjourned.

It was not until 1898 that New York enacted a stringent primary law, one that provided the twin foundations for today's primary system. First, the 1898 law defined as those eligible to participate in a party's primary those who had taken the following oath before a government-employed official and had the record of that oath included on the government-maintained voter register:

> I am in general sympathy with the principles of the party; that it is my intention to support generally at the next election, state or national, the nominees of such party for state or national offices; and that I have not enrolled with or participated in any primary election or convention of any other party since the first day of last year.

The principle of the "closed" primary, the concomitant system of party enrollment, and a long lead time to prevent raiding were thus established and remain intact to this day.

The other important feature of the 1898 law was that government-employed election officials, the same ones who supervised the general elections, were now given complete charge of the primary balloting process. That process was defined to include the specification of the time when primaries for all parties would be held (the seventh Tuesday before general election day); the specification of place, i.e., convenient voting stations; the distribution of official ballot paper on which the competing party factions could print their lists of proposed delegates; and, finally, the administration of the balloting on election day. What had begun as a private *meeting* had thus been transformed into a government-administered *process* of enrollment and balloting. What was to become the most distinctive feature of American politics, the primary election, had been established.

New York State had little over a decade of experience under the new, indirect system before it changed to direct primaries in 1911. It is important to stress, nevertheless, that the indirect system featured numerous instances of spirited contests for convention delegates, with the publicized acknowledgement that at stake was the convention nomination of one candidate over another, or of one faction's candidates over those of another. Thus the indirect primary system seemed able to yield its intended result of allowing the parties' rank-and-file *indirectly* to help choose the parties' nominees, even though the ballot contained only the names of delegate candidates and not the names of the candidates for public office whom they favored.

## The Direct Primary

If New York led the way in 1866 by enacting legislation designed to curb abuses in the system of indirect primaries, it lagged behind other states in the enactment of direct primary legislation. Wisconsin pointed the way in 1903 with the passage of the nation's first statewide primary law, soon to be followed by other large states such as California, Illinois, Michigan, and Ohio. Under the new laws the rank-and-file party members would go to the polls on primary election day and choose not convention delegates but the actual party nominees for the general election.

In New York, however, both major political parties resisted this tide of reform sentiment as long as they could. When they finally were forced to enact a direct primary law in 1911, the law which emerged from the legislature was so faulty that, in the eyes of the critics, it was worse than no law at all. It was not until 1913 that the legislature, meeting in special session, finally enacted a direct primary law which satisfied the reformers and which remains basically intact to this day.

## The Challenge Primary, 1911–1913

In order better to understand the 1913 legislation, it is necessary first to examine the law enacted in 1911. That law established what today would be called a "challenge primary" system.

The idea of the challenge primary had been formulated by Charles Evans Hughes when he was governor of New York (1907–10). It reflected Hughes' assessment of the experience other states had had under the new direct primary sytem.[6] That experience had shown that the party organization, rather than sitting idly by and allowing the rank-and-file membership to choose between competing contenders for the party nomination, would instead meet in a convention or a less formal setting, just as before, and decide which person should receive the party nomination. The organization would then use its resources to support that person in the primary election. Accordingly, primary elections had often become battles between the organization and one or more insurgents attempting to defeat the organization's candidate. Governor Hughes reasoned that such pre-primary activity by party organizations could not be stopped and, hence, should be recognized explicitly in the law. Nor *should* such activity be stopped, Hughes reasoned. In contrast to many other reformers of the period who saw political parties as completely "bad," Hughes recognized the constructive role which parties can play in the screening of candidates, as well as in identifying and encouraging able candidates to seek public office. Accordingly, Hughes sought to retain for the party organizations their all-important role in the nomination process, while at the same time simplifying the structure of the organizations in order to make them more accountable to rank-and-file control. Under Hughes' plan, then, which he unveiled at a speech given in Buffalo in 1909, the party committee at the appropriate level (e.g., state committee, legislative district committee) would "designate" a candidate for office. That name would then appear on the primary ballot. Anyone wishing to challenge the designee could do so by gathering signatures on petitions and submitting these to the election board. The choice would then be made by the rank-and-file party members, whose ballot would indicate which of the candidates was the designee.

The Hughes plan was an attempt to find a middle ground between monopoly of the nomination process by the party organization and what Hughes saw as the equally undesirable condition where the party organization would play no part at all. As enacted by the New York legislature in 1911, however, the balance was tipped decidedly in favor of the organization. Rather than challengers being given three weeks to circulate and submit petitions, they were given only five days; and rather than the number of signatures being reasonable, it was deliberately made onerous. Moreover, only the organization was allowed to appoint election-day inspectors. These provisions, when combined with the provisions which Hughes envisaged but to which many fellow-reformers strongly objected—e.g. number-one ballot position for the designee and organization campaign support (including financial support) for the designee—so incensed leaders of the reform movement that the 1911 law came under immediate attack. In 1913, accordingly, the challenge primary was replaced with today's "pure" primary system. It was not until many years later that Hughes' challenge primary idea was permanently adopted by some other states and in 1951 became the basis for a model primary law proposed by the National Municipal League. In 1967, Hughes' own state, New York, finally adopted the challenge primary for nomination of statewide offices (see below).

*Today's System*

The 1913 law, whose provisions operate to this day (except for statewide offices), was designed to even the chances for all contenders: all contenders were now required to gather petitions in order to have their names appear on the primary ballot; the number of signatures required on the petitions was made reasonable; the names of the candidates would appear on the ballot with no indication of which contender (if any) might be favored by the organization; and the organization could spend no money on behalf of any of them.

Despite these changes in the law, the legacy of *designation* remained. First, that term was retained in the law to describe the petitions to be circulated by the primary contestants, to distinguish those petitions from the *nomination* petitions circulated by independents seeking to have their names placed on the general election ballot. More important, the practice of political party organizations "designating" preferred candidates remained as much a part of the candidate selection process as it had before—just as former Governor Hughes would have predicted. This practice could have been prohibited, as ultimately it came to be in other states (although not always successfully),[7] but was not. Indeed, the 1913 law specifically stated that nothing in the act was to be interpreted as preventing a party from holding a state convention.[8] In addition, of course, there was nothing to prevent a party's county committee or district committee from meeting and discussing any topic, including which candidate to back in a primary. From the perspective of the voter, then, the major difference after 1913 was that the ballot did not indicate which primary contestant was favored by the organization;[9] from the perspective of the challenger the major difference was that the obstacles he once faced were now not quite so formidable. These differences notwithstanding, the political parties in New York made it clear that whatever the election law might say, they were unwilling to abandon their traditional role of identifying preferred candidates and doing everything legally in their power to see that these became the parties' nominees on the November ballot.

The frequency of party designations is suggested by a survey conducted by the author in 1978 for nominations for congressional and state legislative seats. The survey was limited to those districts in which a Republican or a Democratic primary contest occurred. Of the 101 contests (of 110) for which replies were received, party designations were reported as being made in all but 17. Reasons for a party organization not designating a preferred candidate include lack of consensus and the attendant fear of splitting the party; the party being so weakly organized and/or the nomination so undesirable that a designation would be meaningless; or, as is now often the case with New York City Democrats, the city-wide or district-wide organization being so factionalized into party clubs that a single party designation is not possible (candidates thus seek club backing).

The process of making party designations varies widely. When the organizational power has been concentrated in a single leader, as was once the case for boroughs and districts within New York City, the process of designation may involve little more than the leader letting it be known whom he favors, perhaps followed by a meeting of committeepersons endorsing the selection(s).[10] When power has not been so concentrated, designation decisions may still be the product of agreement among a relatively small group of leaders, such as the five county leaders in New York City (for designating city-wide offices), or a county leader meeting with his sub-unit (e.g., town or Assembly district) leaders or with prominent party members holding elective office. In other cases, however, designation of candidates has been accomplished through an open meeting of the whole county committee or committee of a subdivision (e.g., legislative district, town), with two committeepersons attending from each election district. These so-called "conventions" may closely resemble nomination conventions, complete with speeches on behalf of rival contenders, the roll call vote, and, finally, acceptance speeches. They are often accompanied by hoopla, occasionally by high drama, and usually by media coverage. Even the Republican organization in Nassau County, generally conceded to be the most disciplined and effective "machine" in the entire state, has chosen to use this seemingly "democratic" method of candidate designation. Although all such meetings are completely outside the scope of the election law, because they are meetings of the county committee the rules of procedures which are laid down in the law—e.g., that a committeeperson's vote be weighted according to the party's gubernatorial vote last recorded in the election district—are followed.

*Frequency of Primary Contests*

The impact of the continuing practice of party designation is reflected in the low incidence of primary contests. Of course, we would not expect there to be a primary contest for every office. A minority party is often lucky if it can find *anyone* to accept its nomination.

It is not surprising, accordingly, that Republican primaries in New York City have always been much less frequent than Democratic primaries, while in other areas of the state the relative frequency of primary contests between the two parties has been precisely the opposite. It also is not surprising that a popular incumbent may encounter no opposition from within his own party when he seeks re-nomination. With such situations discounted, however, we might still reasonably expect competition for, say, one-third of the two major party candidacies (i.e., one-third of twice the number of offices to be filled) if all contenders had a more or less equal chance of success.

In fact, the proportion of primary contests has always been far less than that. A study of the 1916 Democratic and Republican nominations for Congress and the state legislature found that there were primary contests for only about ten percent of the candidacies.[11] A decade later the proportion had fallen to nearer five percent. After an interlude in the 1930s when dissension within New York City's Democratic party led to a sharp increase in primary contests, the proportion again leveled off to about ten percent and remained at that level during the 1940s and 1950s. Indeed, so infrequent had primaries become by that time that in 1959 the election law was amended to allow the polls not to open in those election districts where only one set of designation petitions had been submitted.

Beginning in the 1960s, however, competition for the parties' nominations began to increase, with the proportion of contests for congressional and state legislative nominations reaching a high of over 20 percent in 1976, 1978, and again in 1982.[12] The same tendency was reflected in competition for the odd-year local government nominations.

The increasing within-party competition seemed to have stemmed from three factors. One was that as a result of "one man, one vote" reapportionment a party's nominations had become more desirable in areas once regarded as hopeless. A second probable reason was that new methods of campaigning (e.g., polling and television) had reduced the importance of campaign efforts made by organizational personnel. However, it seems likely that the most important explanation for the increased frequency of primary contests was the decline in party organizational strength and unity. From the beginning the direct primary has been a powerful weapon not only in the hands of "outsiders" but even more so in the hands of a disgruntled faction within the party organization. George Washington Plunkitt was thus correct in seeing primary laws (even indirect primary laws) as a threat to his power as the boss of Tammany Hall.[13] Carmine De Sapio was the last Tammany leader to feel the reality of that threat when in 1961 Mayor Wagner led the so-called "reform" faction of the City's Democratic party in a resounding victory over De Sapio's candidates in the Democratic primary, thus bringing to an end the career of the last of the great Tammany bosses. Since the 1960s such struggles have become more common. The dampening effect of a strong, unified party organization on primary contests can still be seen in an area like Nassau County. Over the period 1970–1980 there were only seven challenges made to the several hundred Republican designations for local, state legislative, and congressional offices. None were successful. In contrast, in neighboring Suffolk, where Republicanism is just as strong but where the Republican organization is more fragmented, there were 27 primary challenges, five of them successful.

*Frequency of Upsets*

If the frequency of primary contests has been far below the expectations of the reformers who demanded the direct primary system of nomination, the frequency of insurgent success must be regarded by them as being totally discouraging. Indeed, the one pattern has fed upon the other: the less the frequency of insurgent success in one year, the less likelihood that the next year anyone will try to challenge the organization's choices. Because the ballot does not indicate which primary candidate is the party designee, the frequency of insurgent success can by surmised only from newspaper accounts. These post-primary accounts have almost invariably stressed the success of the "regulars" against the insurgents, and when there has been an upset that occasion has rightly been hailed as being of historic importance. In the 1978 survey mentioned above, of the 84 primary contests in which one candidate was reported to be the designee, that candidate was victorious in all but 19 instances. (Even that figure is no doubt misleadingly high, since 17 of these instances involved New York City Democrats, and hence the report of party designation is suspect.)

There are a number of factors which help to explain why the organization's designees are usually victorious in primary contests. First, the task of circulating the designee's petitions is done by the network of party committeepersons. Although the petition requirements in the election law are reasonable, they still present a considerable hurdle to anyone lacking an organized team of workers to assist in the process. For the office of mayor of New York City, for example, the requirement is 10,000 signatures; for the office of county executive, 2,000; for Congress, 1,250; for state Senate, 1,000; for state Assembly, 500. Impeding the signature-gathering effort is the requirement that only an enrolled party member living in the jurisdiction (e.g., legislative district) can circulate a petition or can sign a petition and that the signee must indicate on the petition the election district in which he resides. Accordingly, gathering signatures on street corners or shopping centers is impractical, and the advantage goes to the contender who is supported by workers able to go door to door, working from the enrollment books published by the respective county boards of elections.

A related factor which impedes the insurgent is that the courts in New York have traditionally been extremely strict in their interpretation of the election law. Petitions have been invalidated for such seemingly trivial irregularities as the signee omitting his middle initial, the use of "St." instead of "Street," or because a petition lacked a page number. As a result of these potential traps, the signature requirements listed above are unrealistically low. To be safe, a challenger will need at least twice the number mentioned in the law. The distinctiveness of New York's tradition of petition invalidation became apparent in 1976 when Jimmy Carter found New York to be the only state in which he was unable to field a full slate of delegates in the presidential primary, thanks to some of his potential delegates having their petitions invalidated. Again in 1980, Jerry Brown found that only in New York was he unable to get his name included on the primary ballot; he, too, fell victim to a court decision that his petitions were irregular. At least for Carter there was some consolation. The same tradition which resulted in some of his delegates being thrown off the primary ballot resulted in Eugene McCarthy being unable to get his name included on the November election ballot. Had McCarthy been successful, many believe that Carter would have lost New York and, hence, the election, to Ford.

The second advantage enjoyed by the party's designee is that the organization's network of committeepersons, job holders, and the relatives of these party loyalists constitute a significant portion of the electorate bothering to participate in the primary election. From the beginning, low primary turnout has been a disappointment to reformers who believed that the electorate would jump at the chance to participate directly in the selection of their party's nominees. Thus in the very first year of application of the 1913 direct primary law, voter participation, while increasing somewhat from what it had been before, was described by the press as "light." By 1920, the last year in which statewide contests were held and the first year for which statewide enrollment data were available, turnout was a mere 30 percent for the Republicans and 15 percent for the Democrats.[14]

The pattern of low rates of participation has continued. A crowded Democratic primary for mayor of New York City drew a record 45 percent turnout in 1977, but this contrasted with the more typical 32 percent four years previously. Republican county executive races in Nassau and Suffolk counties in 1977 and 1979, respectively, drew a 28 percent turnout. Of 12 congressional primaries held during the decade of the 1960s for which data are available, the average turnout was 33 percent for Republican and 20 percent for Democrat.

Helping to keep participation in New York's primary elections at a low level is the state's extremely "closed" primary system. New York is one of 27 states in the nation to adhere to the so-called "closed" primary system; within that category, however, there is an enormous variation with respect to the ability of "outsiders" to participate in another party's primary. If an enrolled Republican in New York wants to take sides in a forthcoming Democratic primary, his or her official enrollment must be changed in October of the previous year, a full eleven months prior to a fall (September) primary and five to eight months prior to a spring primary (depending on the month it is held). These requirements are the most stringent of any in the nation and stand in vivid contrast to those in other states, e.g., 50 days in New Jersey, 30 days in Massachusetts and California. The second distinctive aspect of New York's closed system relates to the so-called independent voter, i.e., the registered voter who has not officially enrolled in a party. In other states it is fairly easy for these persons to change their minds and enroll in a party when an interesting primary election is approaching. In New Jersey, Massachusetts, and New Hampshire, for example, these independents are able to appear at the polling place on primary election day, declare their party affiliation, and then proceed to cast a ballot in the chosen party's contest.[15] (In Massachusetts, upon exiting from the voting booth the voter can request that his enrollment be changed back again to independent.) In Connecticut, there is a lead time for an independent to enroll in a party, but the period is only 14 days. In New York, in contrast, independents are subjected to the same time requirements, listed above, as pertain to persons changing enrollment from one party to another.

This latter aspect of the election law has become increasingly restrictive in its effect as the proportion of independents within the New York electorate has increased.[16] In the early part of the century that proportion appears to have been well under ten percent, and in 1955 when the first statewide figures became available it was only six percent. As pointed out in chapter one, however, in the mid 1960s the proportion of independents began to increase dramatically, by 1980 reaching over 20 percent in counties such as Westchester, Suffolk, and Rockland. New voters (18-year-olds and new state residents) were clearly responsible for this trend. In Nassau County, for example, where separate records for new voters are tabulated, the proportion of independents among new voters was 35 percent in 1976 and has remained near 30 percent each year since then. Whatever the explanation for these new voter preferences (e.g., youth disillusionment with parties, the new form designed for mail registration), the consequence was that each year fewer and fewer registered voters were eligible to participate in primaries, at the very time when the frequency of primaries was increasing. Those who were eligible to participate, moreover, were more and more representative of an older generation.[17]

## Statewide Office and the Challenge Primary

The 1913 direct primary law applied to nominations for all major public offices in the state. Less than a decade later the most important of these, the statewide offices, were removed from coverage and returned to the indirect-primary-convention system of nomination, and from then until the law was changed once again in 1967, New York remained one of the very few states not to nominate statewide officers by the direct primary method.[18]

A number of reasons appear to have led to the change back to the convention system in 1921. First, direct primaries in general had almost immediately come under attack for not living up to the predictions which had been made for them. Low turnout was especially noted, and in the rural areas where the indirect primary laws had not applied, and hence primary elections had never before been held, low turnout was discussed in the press in terms of the very high per-vote election costs now incurred. The absence of primary competition was also apparent. At the first statewide primary in 1914 there had been nine Democratic contests and seven Republican contests, or 16 contests in all. In the next three statewide elections (1916, 1918, and 1920) the total number of contests fell to four, six, and seven, respectively. Finally, critics of the direct primary system for statewide office noted the high costs of primary campaigning, so that only persons with large financial resources could challenge the favorites of "the bosses." For these reasons, then, the direct primary was not popular, and as early as 1915 the *New York Times* was calling for a return to the convention system of nomination which, the *Times* argued, had provided the state with many exemplary public officials.

*The Convention System*

Under the system begun in 1922, the convention delegates were elected from each Assembly district, as they had been under the old pre-1911 system. As before, only the names of the delegates appeared on the primary ballot, with no indication as to whom they might favor for any of the statewide nominations. Unlike in the earlier period, however, these indirect primary elections now remained non-competitive. Occasionally, in a few districts a rival slate of delegates committed to a particular gubernatorial candidate would challenge the local leadership's slate of uncommitted delegates, but such contests were clearly exceptional. Hence nominations for statewide office at the 1200–1500 delegate conventions were the product of bargaining and agreements reached among the blocs of delegates or, more precisely, among the county leaders who controlled them.[19] Rank-and-file voters played no part.

The convention system of nomination gave the State of New York some of its most illustrious public officials—Governors Al Smith, Franklin D. Roosevelt, Herbert Lehman, Thomas Dewey, Averell Harriman, and Nelson Rockefeller, and Senators Robert F. Wagner, Irving Ives, Jacob Javits, Kenneth Keating, and Robert Kennedy. This record notwithstanding, the convention system came under increasing attack by good government groups, such as the Citizens Union and the League of Women Voters. The fact that by the mid-1960s only one other state (Indiana) had not adopted the direct primary system for nominating statewide officials seemed to confirm the charge that New York was lagging behind the progressivism of the rest of the country. Reflecting this perspective, the *New York Times* now attacked the "old-fashioned party convention, so often run by party bosses from a smoke-filled room."[20] With the imagery of "the bosses" playing as conspicuous a role in New York politics as the bosses themselves ever had, Governor Rockefeller, refusing to allow himself to be labeled as favoring "the bosses," reluctantly signed into law in 1967 the bill which abolished the convention system of nomination.[21]

*The Challenge System*

The system which the bill substituted for it was not the pre-1921 pure primary system. Rather the bill brought into being a version of Hughes' challenge primary: *designation* for statewide office would be made by a party's state committee, but a challenger could force a primary. Nearly 60 years after Hughes had first posed the idea, and after that idea had been adopted as the "model" primary system by the National Municipal League,[22] Governor Rockefeller, posing before the television cameras with the portrait of Governor Hughes behind him, signed into law today's challenge primary system for nominating statewide officials.

However, the 1967 act departed significantly from the idea which Hughes had first proposed. First, in addition to individuals being able to challenge the party's designee by gathering petitions (20,000 signatures, properly distributed throughout the state), a challenger could also get his name on the primary ballot if he was one of the runner-ups at the designation session of the state committee, receiving at least 25 percent of the weighted votes cast. Although this procedure had been mentioned as a feasible variation by the National Municipal League, the wording of the 1967 law was such that the 25-percent threshold applied not just to the final ballot when one candidate received 51 percent of the votes and thus became the party designee, but also applied to any previous ballot. An infinite number of candidates could thus meet the 25-percent requirement. Second, the 1967 law did not provide for the identification of the designee on the primary ballot. Finally, party organizational expenditure on behalf of the designee was prohibited (such a prohibition had long applied to other primaries).

The 1967 law thus completely ignored the purposes behind the Hughes/NML model, which were (1) to make the party organization responsible for choosing a designee whose personal qualities and policy viewpoints were such that the organization could and would identify with them; (2) to allow but not to encourage a challenge to the organization's choice; (3) to give the rank-and-file party voter some guidance when casting the primary ballot; and (4) by offering the designee organizational resources and organizational legitimacy, to prevent nominations from becoming the preserve of those who could afford to wage a primary campaign or who could find financial backing from pressure groups. Thus the only difference between the new "challenge" system and the "pure" primary system long used for offices below the statewide level was that (1) under the new system the designation meeting, popularly called a "convention," was actually prescribed by law and did not have to be held in defiance of legislative intent; and (2) some primary contenders, i.e., the designee and eligible runner-ups, would not have to gather petitions in order to have their names appear on the primary ballot. From the standpoint of the voter, however, the two systems seemed identical; in neither case was he or she presented with a choice clearly structured in terms of party organization versus a challenger.

Despite the prohibition against party expenditure and despite the absence of ballot identification of the designee, the parties in New York could have made the system work in the way the NML model envisaged if they had assumed an active role in primary campaigns as cohesive organizations with a corporate purpose. They did not do so. One reason was that by this time both parties had abandoned the practice of formulating quadrenniel party platforms; one of the bonds which might have united party organization with the party designee had thus been eliminated. Another reason was that by this time television had enormously reduced the significance of the aid which organizational manpower could provide to the designee. Finally, for the Democrats there was another reason why the challenge system did not work as intended— the issue of "bossism." When the Democrats held their first state committee meeting to choose their designee for governor, their choice, Arthur Goldberg, announced to a startled state committee that he wished to renounce the designation so that he would not be considered "a creature of the bosses," and that he would prove that fact by gathering the same 20,000 signatures he would have needed had he not received the party's official designation. In 1976, competition for the Democratic nomination for the U.S. Senate took the form of seeing which contender could win 25 percent of the state committee vote yet *not* win a majority and thus be stuck with the albatross of being labeled the Democratic designee. In 1980, when there were four Democratic candidates for the U.S. Senate nomination, so divided was the party that it was agreed that there should be no designee, and the choice be left up to the voters in the primary. Accordingly, the votes of the state committee were carefully orchestrated to insure that each candidate received only the necessary 25 percent. In addition to the fact that candidates worked hard to avoid it, the worthlessness of the Democratic party's designation was illustrated by the fact that as of 1980, of the 15 challenges which had been made to party designations since the system began, 10 had been successful.

It was not until the early 1980s that the 1967 challenge primary system began to work, at least in one sense, more along the lines intended. In 1982 two Democratic contenders for governor *did* actively seek their party's designation; the issue of "bossism" obviously had receded from the public agenda. The Republicans, too, began to behave differently. Until 1980 that party's disciplined unity had resulted in there having been only one challenge made to a Republican designation, and that one had been unsuccessful. In 1980, however, Alphonse D'Amato successfully challenged the Republican designation of Javits for the U.S. Senate nomination. In 1982 the Republican designees for governor and U.S. senator were also challenged, the latter successfully.

In one important sense, however, the 1982 Republican gubernatorial designation represented the most extreme departure yet from the intent of the Hughes/NML model. The designee, Lewis Lehrman, had never been active in the Republican party and had never before run for public office. Yet by spending several million dollars of his own money on television commercials in the months preceding the meeting of the state committee he established himself as the frontrunner, and a majority of the committee accordingly voted to make him the party's designee. Clearly money and television had replaced party organization as "kingmaker." The rationale for the challenge primary, as articulated by former Governor Hughes, was that the "citizen of ability, well trained and experienced," would *not* seek public office, and certainly he would have "no inclination to spend time and money trying to get" a party's nomination. He would not subject himself "to the annoyance and expense of an open primary."[23] The only way he might be persuaded to make the personal sacrifice of seeking public office would be for the party organization to guarantee its backing against any possible primary challenger. By 1982 this logic had been turned on its head; now it was the outsider who was forcing himself on the organization. Underscoring the complete failure of the 1967 law was the announcement of the Republican state chairman, following the adjournment of the state committee, that he would remain neutral during the subsequent primary campaign (he later recanted). As with the Democrats, the challenge primary had been transformed into a pure primary system.

Had the authors of the 1967 law foreseen that most nominees would be selected not by the state committees but rather in free-for-all primary contests, they might have incorporated into the legislation a provision for a run-off election, as was provided in 1973 for New York City mayorality primaries. By failing to do so the authors left the door opened for party nominees to be the choice of only a relatively small minority of the rank-and-file party voters. Thus in 1970 Richard Ottinger became the Democratic nominee for U. S. Senate with only 39.7 percent of the primary vote in a four-person race; in 1976 Daniel Patrick Moynihan became the senatorial nominee with only 36.4 percent of the vote in a five-person race; and in 1980 Elizabeth Holtzman became the senatorial nominee with only 40.7 percent of the vote in a four-person race.

In one additional respect the 1967 law has been a disappointment: turnout in the statewide primaries has been no greater than the traditionally low turnout for district or local government primary contests (or for the statewide contests during the 1914–1920 period). Thus through 1980 Democratic participation ranged from between 20 and 30 percent of the state's Democratic enrollment; in 1982 it reached 38 percent. The historic Republican Javits-D'Amato contest in 1980 attracted a mere 25-percent turnout.

*Impact of the Challenge Primary*
Despite its failure to achieve its intended goal, the 1967 law has had a profound impact on the politics of the state. If we can assume that most of the Democratic and Republican *designations* made since 1967 would have been convention *nominations* prior to that date, then the fact that as of 1982 there had been 13 successful challenges made under the 1967 system suggested the law's importance. Governors Hugh Carey and Mario Cuomo, Senators Moynihan and D'Amato, and Court of Appeals Justice Jabob Fuchsburg were not the designees of their party's state committee, yet went on to win their party's primary through the challenge procedure and then win again in the general election. The victory of D'Amato over Senator Javits in 1980 was of special interest since it suggested that New York's Republican party, long known as constituting the more liberal wing of the Republican party, had achieved that reputation by virtue of the fact that the state had held on to its convention tradition long after most states had abandoned it and that only by virtue of that mechanism had it been able to nominate such liberal (and vote-getting) Republicans as Rockefeller and Javits.

A second result of the change in nomination procedures has been that the parties are no longer able to guarantee that they will present to the voters in November a slate of candidates for governor, lieutenant governor, attorney general, and comptroller which will be "balanced" in terms of geography, religion, and ethnicity. The consequences of such balancing, if it succeeds in its purpose, is that the party in office is broadly representative of the entire electorate. It used to be that the nominating conventions would attempt to get a balance between candidates from New York City and upstate (i.e., the remainder of the state), as well as among

Protestants, Catholics, and Jews, and among the various ethnic groups. Indeed, the Republicans, whose state committee in effect operated as a nominating convention until 1980, were able to produce such balanced tickets. Thus in 1978 it presented to the voters two downstate suburbanites (Perry Duryea and Bruce Caputo), one upstate suburbanite (Edward Regan) and one New York City resident (Michael Roth), and in doing so balanced off two Protestants with a Catholic and a Jew. In contrast, the Democrats, reaping the fruits of an open primary system, presented to the voters four candidates from New York City (Hugh Carey, Mario Cuomo, Robert Abrams, and Harrison Goldin), two of them Jewish and two of them Catholic.[24]

A third consequence of the 1967 law was predictable: the need for a candidate to find substantial financial backing for the primary campaign. In the first major test of the new law in 1970, the successful challenger for the Democratic senatorial nomination, Richard Ottinger, reported his expenditures as $1.8 million. Lewis Lehrman in 1982 not only spent several million in the campaign leading up to his designation, but spent several million more in the primary, bringing the total spent to nearly $6 million. The demand for the public financing of all campaign expenditures which began to be heard loudly in the 1980s stemmed in major part from this new burden put upon candidates seeking public office.

The final and related result of the introduction of the challenge primary has been that both the Democratic and the Republican parties, as organizations, have lost control over the nomination of candidates for statewide office. While both organizations retain their ability to control most of the nominations for congressional, state legislative, and local government offices, for statewide office they have been shown to be extremely vulnerable to primary challenges or even to the threat of a challenge. In part this vulnerability is a reflection of the fact that the party organizations in the state have always been decentralized; state party leaders have always been much less powerful than county party leaders. Perhaps even more important, statewide office is able to attract sufficient money (the candidate's own or his contributors') to purchase the products of modern technology—television, polling, computer lists—and the statewide constituency is sufficiently large to make these products both practical and necessary.

## Today's Indirect Primaries

The adoption of the challenge primary in 1967 did not completely eliminate the indirect primary from New York politics. The indirect system is still used for nomination for two additional important offices.

*Presidential Primary*
One of these is the national office of the presidency. Prior to 1911 the selection of delegates to the parties' national nominating conventions was ungoverned by state law. In the legislation enacted that year, however, the parties were given the option of continuing their traditional practice of choosing their delegates at their state conventions, or, instead, choosing them through a primary election to be held in the spring of each presidential election year, with the unit of representation being the congressional district. Thus in 1912 New York held its first presidential primary, with only the Republicans taking advantage of the new procedure: a full slate of pro-Taft delegates was opposed by a full slate of pro-Roosevelt delegates. (The Taft forces won, 87 delegates to 7.) An amendment to the election law in 1913 made the primary procedure of delegate selection mandatory for all parties, so that after that date New York was among that very small group of states in the nation having a presidential primary every four years.

In practice, however, after 1912 the presidential primary never worked out as intended. Rather than there being spirited competition for delegate selection, there was no competition whatsoever. In each district the names of only one slate of delegates would appear on the primary ballot, and that would be the slate proposed by the party leaders. Like for the gubernatorial primaries after 1921, delegate selection became a mere formality, and understandably the press gave no coverage to these non-contests. Occasionally in one or two districts there would be challenges by insurgents, disagreeing with the leadership stance (which was usually one of "favorite son" or non-commitment), who favored the nomination of a particular presidential candidate. In 1964, for example, there were instances of challenges by Republican insurgents who favored the nomination of Barry Goldwater, and in 1980 there were districts where supporters of Ronald Reagan challenged delegates pledged to follow the state Republican party's strategy of non-commitment. Challenges such as these, however, were always so few and far between that most New Yorkers were probably unaware that their state was among the few to have a presidential primary, albeit an indirect one.

It was not until the 1970s that the New York presidential primary began to attract some interest. A major reason was a change in the election law, introduced by the Democrats in 1976 and applying to the Democratic primary only, which allowed the names of presidential aspirants to be printed on the primary ballot alongside the name of the delegate candidates supporting them. Together with the large field of presidential contenders that year, this change resulted in the entry of a number of competing slates of delegates in the 1976 primary. Four years later the Democratic primary attracted even more attention, again in part because of a change in the law—a change which, like the first, applied only to the Democratic primary. Now the names of candidates for delegate would be omitted from the ballot; instead only the names of the presidential contenders themselves would appear. Delegates would be chosen at a later date in numbers proportionate to the strength shown by the contenders in the primary balloting. In a procedure which recalled that used a century before, the delegates would be chosen at a gathering of the party rank-and-file voters brought together in a school or other centrally located place within the congressional district. In a historical reversal, *process* had been transformed back again into *meeting*.

*Supreme Court Justices*
The other public office for which the indirect-primary-convention system of nomination is still used is that of state Supreme Court justice. There are several hundred of these 14-year positions distributed among the state's 11 judicial districts. Although this office was subject to the direct primary system of nomination during the period 1913–1921, since 1921 Supreme Court nominations, when required, have been made at specially called judicial district conventions made up of delegates chosen at the primary election. Like for other indirect primaries, however, the theory of rank-and-file control of judicial nominations has never worked out in practice. Competition for the delegate positions is virtually unheard of. The

composition of the judicial conventions, and the nominations made at those conventions, have thus reflected the wishes of a relatively small group of party leaders.

## Conclusion

Political parties are usually defined as organizations which nominate candidates for public office. Other organizations (e.g., interest groups) can articulate policy positions and support candidates for election; it is the nomination of candidates which makes political party organizations distinctive. To what extent do the party organizations in New York perform this function? The best way to answer that question, as of the 1980s, is to treat separately three groups of offices.

The party organizations are at their strongest in nominating candidates for the office of Supreme Court justice. Here the party organizations remain supreme; the "bosses" who control the judicial conventions, held periodically in the state's 11 judicial districts, are as powerful today as they were a century ago. Accordingly, any ambitious lawyer who aspires to one of these prestigious judicial posts is well advised to become active in party affairs, becoming a committeeperson, running first for lesser office, and financially contributing to the party coffers. There is no other way.

At the next level, and almost as secure for the party organizations, are nominations for local government office (city, town, county), state legislative office, and—slightly less secure—congressional office. In locations where these nominations are worth having, the party organization is usually able to see that its designee becomes the nominee, the hopes of the 1913 reformers notwithstanding. Again, anyone aspiring to run for one of these offices is well advised to become active in party affairs, and be satisfied initially with designations for the lower-level offices. Although an insurgent faction within a party organization may sometimes be successful in a primary challenge, the chances for success of an outsider are not very great.

Finally, least secure for the party organizations are the nominations for the statewide offices. Rather than providing a mechanism under which the organizational designees can be challenged, the 1967 reform has been transformed, in practice, into a pure pri-

mary system. For these state-wide offices, however, the pure primary system works very differently than it does for most lower-
level offices. The attractiveness of the offices, plus the large constituency which must be reached, have made modern campaign
technology the key to nomination. That key is available to any
potential candidate with sufficient funds, regardless of his or her
standing with the organization. Accordingly, for the statewide offices a party's nomination may truly be said to be as much in the
hands of the rank-and-file party enrollees as it is in the hands of
the party organization and its leaders.

# Notes

1. The only towns where elected offices are subject to party primaries are those
which are located in counties with populations of at least 750,000. As of 1970 only
56 of the state's 931 towns fell under this requirement. In many towns, however,
one or more of the parties have exercised their option of requesting official primaries (administered by the respective county boards of elections), a procedure which
allows a town's party leader(s) to avoid taking sides when there are rival contenders
for the nomination. In most village elections the official parties take no part; hence
their freedom to choose nominees at this level of government in any way they wish
is of little consequence.

2. Even the method for selecting candidates for presidential electors is specified
in the election law: selection by the party's state committee.

3. *Democracy and the Party System,* Macmillan (New York, 1910); the complete
two-volume work on European and American parties was published in 1902.

4. The early history of primary legislation in New York and other states is
described in Charles Edward Merriam, *Primary Elections,* University of Chicago
Press (Chicago, 1908).

5. A.C. Bernheim, "Party Organizations and Their Nomination to Public Office
in New York City," *Political Science Quarterly,* Vol. 3 (1888), pp. 99–122.

6. Hughes' views are to be found in "New York's Electoral Reform," *National
Municipal Review,* Vol. 4 (1914), pp. 134–35; and his 1920 presidential address to
the National Municipal League, found in ibid., Vol. 10 (1921), pp. 23–31.

7. In New Jersey, for example, attempts to outlaw organizational endorsements
have been completely unsuccessful. See Alan Rosenthal and John Blydenburgh,
*Politics in New Jersey,* Eagleton Institute, Rutgers (New Brunswick, 1975), Ch. 5.

8. This point is discussed in Schuyler T. Wallace, "Pre-Primary Conventions,"
*The Annals,* Vol. 106 (1923), p. 101.

9. Such identification continues to characterize the ballot in those five states
which today use a version of the challenge primary—viz., Connecticut, Utah, Colorado, North Dakota, and Rhode Island.

10. Thus a 1946 study of New York City reported that for city-wide office "the
nominees are generally named at a caucus of the leaders of the five (county) orga-

nizations and 'ratified' in the primaries. At the last Democratic County Committee meeting in New York [i.e., Manhattan], the two thousand members ratified, unanimously, by a voice vote, all resolutions and personnel recommendations presented by Leader Edward V. Loughlin." See Hugh A. Bone, "Political Parties in New York City," *American Political Science Review*, Vol. 40 (1946), p. 273. Designation procedures in New York are also discussed in Edward N. Costikyan, *Behind Closed Doors*, Harcourt, Brace and World, (New York, 1966), Chs. 7–9; and Roy V. Peel, *The Political Clubs of New York City*, Ira J. Friedman, Inc. (Port Washington, 1968), Ch. 14. Albany County provides another good example of a strong Democratic organization. See Frank S. Robinson, *Machine Politics: A Study of Albany's O'Connells*, Transaction Books, (New Brunswick, N.J., 1977), Ch. 23.

11. H. Feldman, "The Direct Primary in New York State," *American Political Science Review*, Vol. 11 (1917), pp. 494–518. Determining the number of primary contests has always been difficult since the only official records are dispersed among the state's 58 election boards (New York City plus 57 counties). The frequency of primary contests in this paragraph has been gleaned from the *New York Times* accounts, where the coverage of non-City contests has usually been incomplete. Only beginning in the 1970s, with the establishment of the state board of elections, has there been available a centralized record of primary contests for congressional and state legislative seats.

12. The proportion fell back to 13 percent in 1980, still high by comparison with earlier decades.

13. William L. Riordon, *Plunkitt of Tammany Hall*, E.P. Dutton (New York, 1963), pp. 81–83.

14. See Louise Overacker, "The Operation of the State-Wide Direct Primary in New York State," *The Annals*, Vol. 106 (1923), pp. 142–147.

15. The significance of the Massachusetts system was illustrated in 1978 when Senator Edward Brooks, up for re-election, aimed his unsuccessful primary election appeal at Republicans and independents, as well as at Democrats whom he urged to change registration by the 30-day deadline; and again in 1980, when over 10,000 Republicans changed their registration to independent, prior to the 30-day deadline, and then proceeded to participate in the Democratic presidential primary.

16. Although there are some states with a higher percentage of registered independent voters, the consequences in those states are not as great as in New York. As we have seen, the Massachusetts total of 40 percent independents is rather meaningless. Connecticut's proportion of 36 percent is diminished in significance by the fact that because of the challenge primary system (only contenders receiving 20 percent of a convention's vote are able to challenge the convention winner), primary contests are very infrequent. Colorado, with 37 percent independents, has a similar challenge system, as well as non-partisan local elections. These figures are taken from *The Almanac of American Politics*, E.P. Dutton (New York), 1980 or 1976 editions.

17. One final feature of New York election practice may be mentioned as making insurgency success in primaries unlikely. The wide use of voting machines in primary elections (their use is mandated only in general elections) has the effect of discouraging voters from writing in the names of their preferred candidate in the event that the candidate has been unable to meet the petition requirements. Such write-in votes are much easier where paper ballots are used than they are with

New York's voting machines, where there is no pencil furnished and there are no visible instructions on the machine telling the voter how to exercise the write-in option.

Despite these obstacles, write-in votes are clearly envisaged in the election law: where only one set of valid petitions has been submitted and, thus, (since 1959) normally there would be no election held, a voter may petition that the polls be open so that write-in votes can be cast. There are always a few districts each year where such petitions are filed, although these petitions, like other petitions in New York, are subject to close scrutiny.

18. The 1911 primary law had also omitted statewide offices from coverage. Prior to the change in the state constitution in 1925 statewide offices included not only governor, lieutenant governor, attorney general, comptroller, Court of Appeals justices, and U.S. senator, but also offices of secretary of state, treasurer, and state engineer.

Once the governorship and other statewide offices became four-year terms beginning in 1938, a party's state committee, rather than a delegate convention, was allowed to make the nomination for an office (e.g., U.S. senator) becoming vacant in a non-gubernatorial election year.

19. For an account of the Democratic conventions, see Costikyan, Chs. 10–13.

20. Editorial, "Direct Primary for New York," May 3, 1967, p. 44. The *Times'* previous position will be found in the editorial of February 25, 1915, p. 8.

21. The episode is recounted by Alan Hevesi in *Legislative Politics in New York State,* Praeger (New York, 1975), p. 165.

22. See Joseph P. Harris, *A Model Direct Primary System,* National Municipal League (New York, 1951).

23. "The Fate of the Direct Primary," *National Municipal Review,* Vol. 10 (1921), p. 27.

24. For a more complete analysis of ethnic balance, see Robert Marcus, "The Ethnic Connection in New York Politics," *Empire State Report,* April 20, 1981, pp. 255 ff.

# 3.

# Cross-Endorsement, Ballot Format, and New York's Multi-Party System

**A**LTHOUGH THE United States is usually spoken of as having a two-party system, New York State stands out as the conspicuous exception. As indicated more fully in chapter one, by all available standards of measurement the minor parties in New York are by far the most institutionalized of those of any state in the nation. What accounts for this distinctiveness? In part the answer may be found in the relatively easy requirement imposed on parties in order for them to become officially recognized. Fifty thousand votes for a gubernatorial candidate is less than one percent of the total vote. In neighboring Connecticut, by contrast, the requirement is 20 percent.[1] But there is another, more fundamental explanation for New York's multi-party system, one which accounts for the proliferation not only of the officially-recognized minor parties but also of the many non-official parties which spring up at most elections, gaining access to the ballot through the petition route. That explanation is the provision of the state's election law which allows the practice of so-called "cross-endorsement."

In New York that term describes a system whereby (1) two or more political parties are able to nominate the same candidate for a public office, and (2) each of the several nominating parties is able to list the joint candidate's name on its own separate row or column on the voting machine, with the candidate's vote total being calculated by adding together the votes he or she receives at these several ballot positions. Only a few other states have ever allowed the first of these practices, joint nominations (e.g., California until 1959); and even fewer have combined that practice with the second, multiple ballot placement. Today, outside New York only in Connecticut and Vermont is either practice allowed.[2] In New York the combined practice of multiple nomination and multiple ballot placement, buttressed by certain other distinctive features of the election law to be discussed, has had the effect of (1) facilitating the attainment by minor parties of official party status; (2) placing minor parties in the position of holding the balance of power, thereby nullifying the "winner take all" theory of minor party demise; (3) undermining the "wasted vote" theory of minor party demise; (4) allowing voters the luxury of supporting a major party's candidate without supporting the candidate's party; and (5) protecting and enhancing the power of the minor parties and their leadership. It will be shown that these consequences were unforeseen and that the several provisions of the election law which have encouraged the growth of minor parties were not intended to have that result.

## Official Party Status

As pointed out in chapter one, New York's election law, like those of most other states, grants easier ballot access (either no petition requirements or less stringent requirements) to parties which are officially recognized than those which are not. It is thus to a party's great advantage to gain official recognition by polling at least 50,000 votes for its gubernatorial candidate.

A very modest requirement in its own right, cross-endorsement can render the 50,000 vote threshold meaningless. A minor party can borrow on the prestige of a major party's gubernatorial candidate by nominating that candidate as its own. (Prior to 1947 the minor party did not need major party approval to do so.) Of the 12 minor parties which have gained official recognition in this century, three initially gained such status, and many have retained it, by this method.[3] Today's Liberal party has only once fielded its own gubernatorial candidate; the Conservative party initially won official recognition with its own candidate for governor (as did Right to Life in 1978), but since 1974 has endorsed the Republican nominee.

The crucial role of separate ballot placement in spawning minor parties can be seen by noting what happened when the ballot format was modified in 1913. The New York legislature yielded to reformist pressures and abandoned the party-column ballot, with its circle at the top for straight-party voting, in favor of the office-block ballot format. But the design of the new ballot added a new complexity to a cross-endorsed candidacy: should the name of the cross-endorsed candidate be printed several times, as it had been with the party-column ballot, or only once? For the office of governor, New York answered this question by printing the name only once, but printing to the left of the name a series of party emblems and adjacent voting squares (Figure I). At the first election held with the new ballot (1914), it became apparent that voters tended to place their "X" in the first square immediately to the left of the candidate's name, a pattern which the architects had obviously not foreseen since that location was initially given to the square of a minor party. Noting this pattern, both major parties made sure that next time their respective emblems and voting squares occupied the favored location (as shown in Figure I) and not the extreme left-side position as in 1914. The result was dramatic: in the 1916 election three of the minor parties which had retained official status in 1914 lost that status, never to be heard from again.[4] In 1922 the Farmer Labor party (which had attained official status in 1920 by running its own gubernatorial candidate) suffered a similar fate when it endorsed the Socialist gubernatorial candidate. Clearly, the office-block ballot format was incompatible with minor-party strategy of using another party's candidate to attain official recognition,[5] and the period following 1916 marks the low point of minor-party strength in New York during this century. Only the Socialist and the Prohibition parties, running their own gubernatorial candidates, survived the change in ballot format. It was not until 1936 that there was another major-minor party cross-endorsement at the gubernatorial level: in that year the American Labor party gained official status by endorsing the Democratic nominee, Herbert Lehman.

By that time, however, another change had occurred in New York's ballot format: the introduction of the voting machine. Like the change in 1913, the change to voting machines had unforeseen

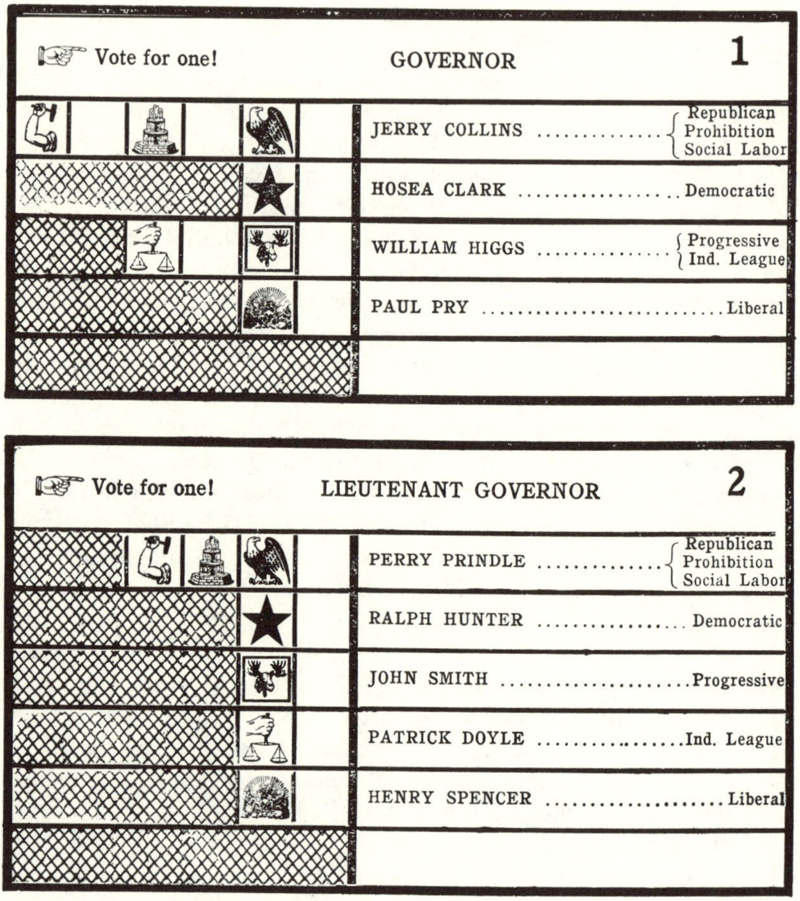
Vote for one! GOVERNOR 1

JERRY COLLINS .............. Republican / Prohibition / Social Labor

HOSEA CLARK .................. Democratic

WILLIAM HIGGS .............. Progressive / Ind. League

PAUL PRY ......................... Liberal

Vote for one! LIEUTENANT GOVERNOR 2

PERRY PRINDLE .............. Republican / Prohibition / Social Labor

RALPH HUNTER ................ Democratic

JOHN SMITH ..................... Progressive

PATRICK DOYLE ................ Ind. League

HENRY SPENCER ............... Liberal

Figure 1: Plate from 1916 election law.

consequences. As pointed out in chapter one, presented on a voting machine, the office-block format is virtually indistinguishable from the party-column of old since all of a party's candidates are located on a separate, identifiable horizontal row or, as in New York City, in a separate vertical column. Consequently, when minor party supporters vote for their party's gubernatorial *candidate,* they are also voting for the *party,* helping the party reach the 50,000 vote threshold. Voting machines were only sparsely used in 1913; by 1938 they were compulsory throughout the state. The successful tactic of the ALP in endorsing the Democratic gubernatorial nominee in 1936—the first such success in nearly 20 years—is thus understandable. Since 1936 all gubernatorial elections but two have been marked by a minor party attaining official recognition by endorsing a major party's candidate for governor, thanks to the separate ballot placement which the introduction of the voting machine made possible.

## Other Offices and Separate Ballot Placement

The impact of voting machines on minor party growth was more profound as that change affected voting for offices other than governor. With one exception,[6] for these offices the 1913 law did *not* provide a series of emblems and voting squares. Rather, as illustrated by the lieutenant governor ballot in Figure I, only one square was provided. As in California in the days of its system of "cross-filing" (abolished in 1959), when a candidate for office was nominated by more than one party, the ballot simply listed the names of those parties beside the candidate's name. The voter could express a candidate preference, but not a party preference.

Although the disappearance of three of New York's minor parties with the 1916 election prevents us from assessing the independent effect on minor parties of this aspect of the 1913 ballot-format change, the experience of New York City is suggestive. As far back as before the turn of the century elections in the City had featured contests between Tammany Democratic candidates and candidates backed by a "fusion" of three or four non-official political parties (e.g., Citizens Union), each of which would petition for a separate ballot column in which to list the common slate of fusion candidates. Sometimes the Republicans would join the fusion movement, thus adding still another column in which the names of the joint candidates would appear. Beginning in 1917, however, the first City election with the office-block ballot paper, the coalition was reduced to only two non-official parties, which shared the single voting square. In the following three City elections all such minor parties disappeared completely from the ballot; elections returned to being virtual straight two-party fights between Democrats and Republicans. Not until 1933, *the second election with voting machines,* was the fusion idea revived by Fiorello LaGuardia, who ran that year on the Republican and Fusion party columns on the voting machine. Every City election since then has featured various combinations of joint candidacies (often styled "fusion") of official parties, or of official and non-official parties. Mayor Koch's 1981 self-styled "fusion" candidacy (Democrat and Republican columns) is a recent example.

In addition to this historical evidence, the importance of separate ballot placement to the nourishment of minor parties in New York City was clearly illustrated in 1911 when the Tammany forces in the state legislature were able to push through a law designed to stop the fusion movement. Rather than outlaw multiple nominations, the law simply held that the name of the candidate would appear on the ballot in one column only; in the other columns there would be a note informing the voter where he could find the name of the endorsed candidate. In the opinion of the party professionals, then, separate ballot placement for each of the minor parties had been the key to these parties' successful coalition efforts. Amidst cries of outrage from good government forces, the Court of Appeals found the 1911 act *ultra vires* under the New York constitution.[7]

Comparative analysis of states likewise suggests the importance of multiple ballot placement in nourishing minor party growth. Three other states—California, Massachusetts, and Pennsylvania—allowed *joint nominations* to appear on their ballot during much of the first half of the century, but only Pennsylvania's ballot allowed for *multiple ballot placement*. Pennsylvania was the only state where most of the joint nominations were between a major and minor party; in the other two states the joint nominations were almost exclusively Republican–Democratic.[8]

*Balance of Power*

What makes separate ballot placement so important to minor party growth? One answer is that it allows a minor party to preserve its autonomy in the eyes of the voters. More important, it makes possible post-election arithmetic. Today when a minor party in New York endorses a Republican or a Democratic candidate, post-election arithmetic can reveal how much the party contributed to the joint nominee's vote total; and when the minor party has run its own candidate, analysis can show how much the minor party *might have* helped a major party candidate had only a joint candidacy been agreed upon. Both types of post-election analysis are, of course, based on a certain degree of speculation. As shown below, there is evidence that the minor party vote for a joint candidacy often reaches the size it does only because voters know that they are not wasting their votes. Be that as it may, the minor parties have been successful in selling their self-serving interpretations of election outcomes. Pointing to the last election, minor party leaders can offer the lure of the party's ballot line either to an individual Republican or Democratic candidate, or to the Republican or Democratic leadership at the state, county, or town level, in which case the endorsement agreement (critics call them "deals") may cover an entire range of candidacies for all offices to be filled by the election. Although occasionally the inducement offered to the minor party is to allow it to run one of its own members on the major party ballot line, normally the inducement takes the form of patronage (judgeships have been the favorite target of Liberal strategists) and policy promises (the death penalty has been an issue of utmost importance to Conservatives; anti-abortion is the cause of Right to Life).

The founders of the Conservative party clearly perceived the balance-of-power strategy made possible by the state's election law, as the following extract from the party's 1962 proposal makes clear:

> We envision the creation of a fourth political party in New York State, the Conservative Party. Like the present Liberal Party, it would *exercise leverage* upon the major political parties by endorsing and working for candidates from either party whose views paralleled its own, and running its own candidates where acceptable major party candidates were not put forth.[9]

The Right to Life party was formed for the same reason. According to a party spokesman, the purpose of the party is "not to have our own people elected to office. We leave politics to the politicians. We would prefer to endorse rather than run our own people."[10] This being the party's purpose, it is understandable that while anti-abortion forces are strong throughout the nation, only in New York have they formed their own party. The party has taken the cross-endorsement system to a new level by requiring a signed anti-abortion pledge of all candidates it endorses.

For Right to Life the temptation to form a new party was greater than it had been for the Liberals and Conservatives before them. The more parties there are, the more fragmented the vote, and hence the greater bargaining power of each. The multi-party system feeds on itself. Whereas in the ten-year period preceding the entry of the Conservative party into New York politics, the Liberal vote was crucial in determining the outcome of 81 congressional and/or state legislative contests, in the ten-year period following the Conservative entry the number rose to 104. Said another way, today the large majority of instances where the Liberal vote is crucial are precisely the same instances where the Conservative vote is crucial. Political scientists normally think of the "winner take all" aspect of plurality election systems as an impediment to third party survival: a third party's candidates in the various districts may make showings which are respectable but not good enough to defeat the major party plurality-winners, and after a while the third party will fade away. In New York it is precisely this aspect of the plurality election system which makes third party survival possible: a major party's loss of a district, though by only a handful of votes, is still a loss, and the handful of votes is there for those who wish to bid for them.

The cynical game which the minor parties play in New York was clearly illustrated in 1980 when the Liberal party agreed to run John Anderson as its presidential candidate *provided that* Anderson not run also on the independent line his backers were proposing. In other words, the goal of the Liberal party was to win the maximum number of votes for its ballot line, not the maximum votes for candidate Anderson. In that goal the party was successful; the post-election arithmetic allowed the party leaders to boast that they had prevented Carter from carrying New York State, the 468,000 Liberal-Anderson votes being greater than the margin by which Reagan carried the state.

As Table I indicates, 1980 was not the first time the Liberal Party had been crucial in determining important election outcomes.[11] In 1960 John F. Kennedy carried New York State and thus defeated Nixon for the presidency only with the help of the Liberal vote. Twice the Liberal vote has been crucial in determining the outcome of gubernatorial elections (including 1966 when the party ran its own candidate), and five times it has been crucial in determining outcomes of a U.S. senate race (including times the party has endorsed the Republican candidate). Not until 1980 was the Conservative party able to boast of accomplishments such as

**Table I.** Separate, Cross-Endorsed, and Crucial Candidacies

| Office | Liberal Party (1948–80) | | | Conservative Party (1964–80) | | |
|---|---|---|---|---|---|---|
| | Separate Candidates | Cross Endorsed | Crucial to Outcome | Separate Candidates | Cross Endorsed | Crucial to Outcome |
| President | 1 | 8 | 2 | 0 | 3 | 1 |
| Governor | 1 | 7 | 2 | 2 | 2 | — |
| Other Statewide* | 3 | 24 | 8 | 10 | 4 | 1 |
| Legislative (Cong., State Legislature) | 1532 (40%) | 2258 (60%) | 149 (3.9%) | 830 (42%) | 1154 (58%) | 244 (12.3%) |

*U.S. Senator, Comptroller, Attorney General
Note: To facilitate comparison, tabulation of Liberal party legislative candidacies begins with 1964.

these; in that year, thanks to the fragmentation provided by Liberal strategy and the new Right to Life party, Conservatives were able to claim that their vote, too, had been crucial in determining both the presidential and senatorial outcome.

At the congressional and state legislative levels, as well as at the local government level, the Conservative party has always played a more crucial role than the Liberals. This is due to the fact that much of the Conservative vote is concentrated in suburban areas where a relatively small margin separates Republican and Democratic strength. In 1968 and 1970 the Republicans won control of the state Assembly (and thus were able to draw the reapportionment map) only because of Conservative endorsements in a number of close districts. Liberal votes, in contrast, are concentrated in New York City, where Democratic candidates can usually win without help from the Liberal line.

Table I also shows the proportion of separate and cross-endorsed minor party candidates for statewide and district offices. As can be seen, both parties rely heavily on cross-endorsed candidates rather than their own separate candidacies with the Liberal party usually backing Democratic candidates and the Conservative party Republican candidates.[12] Political parties are usually defined as organizations which nominate candidates to run for public office; other politically-involved organizations are called pressure groups. The minor parties in New York are thus better described by the latter term.

It is very clear why the minor parties do not nominate their own candidates. The only time the Conservatives have been successful with their own candidate was in 1970 when James Buckley won the three-way race for the U.S. Senate, thanks to the backing from President Nixon and other Republicans who thought the Republican nominee was "too liberal." The Liberal party has never won a statewide office with its own candidate, and not until the late 1970s, when it won three legislative seats, did it manage to be victorious at this level of government. Here again, however, victories were made possible only because insurgents from a major party, in this case the Democrats, backed the Liberal candidate. These few victories would not have been sufficient to keep New York's minor parties from withering; what has prevented that fate has been their ability to endorse major party candidates. The Conservative party especially has come to rely on this method of survival; in the early 1960s some 70 percent of its legislative candidates ran separately on the ballot, but by 1980 the proportion had fallen to 12 percent.

## Psychological Advantages of Separate Ballot Placement

*The "Wasted Vote" Theory*
In addition to the "winner take all" feature, plurality election systems have been said to inhibit minor party growth because of the psychological factor: since there are no rewards for coming in second in a district, would-be minor party supporters are reluctant to "waste" their vote in what is almost surely a losing cause. Survey data in both Britain and the United States have confirmed the validity of this theory.[13]

New York's cross-endorsement system undermines this psychological dynamic in two ways. First, minor party supporters may know that their party's separate candidate for, say, Congress, will receive only a small fraction of the district vote—the Liberal or Conservative district vote hardly ever exceeds ten percent—, but since the size of the vote determines future negotiating strength, the vote is not wasted. More important, in the event that their party does endorse a major party candidate, the minor party supporters can "have it both ways": they can vote for a probable winner while at the same time voting for their party. Evidence of the working of this second psychological dynamic is provided by the fact that minor party candidates who run separately normally poll fewer votes than do those candidates who run cross-endorsed. A dramatic illustration of this tendency occurred in 1980 when Right to Life candidate for President Ellen McCormack polled only 24,000 votes while her party's candidate for U.S. senator, Alfonse D'Amato, who was also the candidate of the Republican and Conservative parties, polled 152,000 votes on the Right to Life line of the ballot. Thus minor party supporters appear to be willing to vote for their party's candidate only if to do so will not be "throwing away" their vote.[14]

*Multiple Option*

The cross-endorsement system allows the supporters of major party candidates a luxury, too: they can vote for the candidate they like without voting for the party they dislike. One of the reasons that labor leaders in New York City founded the American Labor party in 1936 was to allow anti-Tammany Democrats the option of voting for Roosevelt's re-election that year without, however, supporting the Democratic organization.[15] Nearly 275,000 selected this option. There have been many other notable instances of this tactic. As suggested above, the various fusion movements which have dotted New York City's political history have been coalitions of Republicans and various reform groups, each of which would list the common slate of fusionist candidates on its own separate place on the ballot. Tammany itself employed this tactic in 1909 when it listed its candidates on eight separate columns of the ballot, featuring such labels as "Liberty, Equality, and Justice," and "Public Ownership and Control." The first statewide candidate to employ this tactic was Nelson Rockefeller, who ran for governor in 1970 not only as a Republican but also on a line carrying the title "Civil Service Independents." Lewis Lehrman in 1982 also adopted this strategy, running for governor on a separate "Independent" line in addition to his Republican and Conservative lines. (Rockefeller's extra line, attracting some 46,000 votes, came close to polling the required 50,000 votes needed for official party recognition, and a widely believed rumor is that only high-level "auditing" of the votes prevented the recorded total from reaching that threshold.) Although the additional votes provided by an extra ballot line usually constitute only a small fraction of the candidate's total vote, in close elections these increments may spell the difference between victory and defeat. As a result, in every election at the district and local level there are always a number of candidates who will take the trouble (by gathering signatures on petitions) to get their names placed on an additional ballot line designated with the label "independent" or some variant thereof. Multiple ballot placement thus continues to be the means by which voters who refuse to support one of the major political parties—with their strong organizations, patronage, and sometimes corruption—can still support known and viable candidates for public office.[16]

As already indicated, the courts in New York state have been extremely protective of the voter's right to the multiple ballot option, and accordingly have struck down various legislative attempts to outlaw joint nominations or restrict them to a single ballot line. In the case most often cited, decided in 1910, the state's highest court ruled that the New York constitution guarantees to voters the right "to choose public officers on whatever principle or dictated by whatever motive they see fit."[17] Bolstering the court's protective behavior, various good government groups have likewise defended multiple nominations and multiple ballot placement, arguing that a change in the system would play into the hands of the "bosses." For example, the Citizens' Union once cited the example of Tom Dewey, who never would have been elected in 1937 as New York City's district attorney—a post which led to scandals being uncovered and a political career launched—had he not been able to combine the votes he polled on the Republican and American Labor party lines of the ballot.

## Protection of Minor Parties and Their Leadership

Prior to 1947 New York's election law was similar to the old California law in that there was no prohibition against a person "cross filing," i.e., filing petitions with the election board for entry into more than one party's primary. In California this system resulted in Republicans and Democrats successfully "raiding" each other's primaries, i.e., entering and winning the other major party's primary and then appearing on the November ballot as the nominee of both major parties. Earl Warren won the California governorship this way in 1946. In New York, in contrast, raids by the two major parties on each other's primaries (or on minor party primaries) never seem to have been attempted.[18] Nor, prior to the 1940s were there more than a handful of instances where a minor party attempted to raid a major party's primary. In 1942, however, Vito Marcantonio, Chairman of the American Labor party, filed primary petitions for both the Republican and Democratic nominations in New York's 18th Congressional District and in the subsequent primaries won both nominations by defeating the respective Republican and Democratic organization-backed candidates. To stop further raids, a Republican legislature amended the election law to provide that when a candidate files petitions for a party's nomination his official voter registration card must show that he is enrolled in that party. Since the only way a person can become a party's nominee on the November ballot is by filing primary petitions (the one exception today is for the Supreme Court nomination), and since a voter can be enrolled in only one party at a time, this Wilson-Pakula Law might have brought an end to New York's cross-endorsement system. But the law contained one important qualification: a candidate could file for another party's primary (and if uncontested, automatically become that party's nominee) if he received the written authorization, filed with the election board, of that party's executive committee at the appropriate jurisdictional level (e.g., state, county, district).

Intended as a brake on minor party growth and hailed as a step to "preserve the two-party system," the Wilson-Pakula Law in fact paved the way for precisely the opposite result. First, the anti-raid protection afforded by the law came to be valued at least as much by the minor parties as by the major ones. Today, as the distinctiveness of the Liberal and Conservative appeal has faded, it is only the 1947 law which has prevented Democrats and Republicans from entering these minor parties' primaries. Indeed, in the case of judicial offices, which were omitted from coverage by the 1947 law, such raids do in fact occasionally occur. Raids on each other's primaries by Conservative and Right to Life parties would also be a likely possibility. Equally important, the "authorization" provision of the 1947 law came to be used not, as intended, by the major parties' executive committees to permit in exceptional circumstances the entry of minor party candidates into their primaries, but rather by the minor parties' executive committees authorizing the entry of major party candidates into theirs. That is, the law provided the legal foundation for today's cross-endorsement agreements whereby in return for specified patronage or policy favors the minor party leadership agrees (1) not to contest its *own* primary; (2) to authorize the entry into its primary of only one candidate from the major party, the one backed by the major party organization; and (3) to fight any insurgent within its own ranks who tries to upset the arrangement with a primary challenge. In making such agreements possible, the 1947 law thus enormously enhanced the power and prestige of minor parties and their leaders (such as the late Liberal leader Alex Rose). Indeed, by formalizing and legitimizing the annual bargaining sessions, the law enhanced the power and prestige of the leaders of *all* parties, major and minor alike.[19]

When combined with another feature of the election law, the 1947 act added to the power of the minor parties and their leadership in another way. Unlike the law in most states (including California during the period when cross-filing was allowed), a candidate who loses his own party's primary in New York may still be the nominee of another party. Accordingly, the leaders of minor parties in New York are able to come to the rescue of a Republican or a Democratic candidate who is rejected by his own party's rank-and-file voters. The reward to the minor party which makes the rescue possible by signing the necessary "authorization" may be enormous. One of the most dramatic examples was seen in 1969, when New York City Mayor John Lindsay lost his own Republican party primary but, winning uncontested the Liberal party primary, went on to win re-election in November as that party's nominee. The often-heard quip during the following year was that there was hardly a Liberal in the state who did not hold a job in the Lindsay administration.[20] A similar scenario was followed in Buffalo in 1977 when a Democratic contestant, defeated in his own party's mayorality primary, went on to win the election in November as the Conservative party candidate. In 1980 Senator Jacob Javits hoped for a similar outcome; defeated in his own Republican primary, he ran for re-election as the Liberal party's candidate. In this instance, however, the rescue operation failed; Javits lost in the general election.[21]

Perhaps the most powerful weapon in the hands of the minor party leaders, however, has been their ability to "raid" the major party designations. Protected by the Wilson-Pakula Law, the minor party leaders have been able to threaten the major parties with separate candidacies unless the major parties designate candidates who are acceptable. The 1982 Republican gubernatorial designation of Lewis Lehrman was a conspicuous example. If the major parties refuse to accede to such threats, the minor party leadership can still play a role in the subsequent major party primary contest. Thus Mario Cuomo's primary victory over Democratic designee Edward Koch in 1982 was due, in part, to the role played by Liberal leaders in the Cuomo primary election campaign. Also in that year the Conservative party leaders were conspicuously active in the successful primary campaign waged by challenger Florence Sullivan against the Republican designee for the U.S. senatorial nomination. In that campaign the Conservative party expended its own funds on behalf of the Sullivan candidacy, something which the Republican party was prohibited by the election law from doing on behalf of its own candidate. Vito Marcantonio could not have done better.

## The Minor Parties and Legislative Outcomes

There is no way we can show conclusively that public policies in New York have been influenced by pressures exerted by the state's minor parties. What we can show is the relationship between roll call votes which express a so-called "liberal" position, roll call votes which express a so-called "conservative" position, and the pattern of Liberal party and Conservative party endorsement. For this purpose a useful tool of analysis is provided by the scores awarded to congressmen by the Americans for Democratic Action and scores awarded to state legislators by the New York Civil Liberties Union; the higher a legislator's score on these indices, the more his roll-call votes have coincided with the positions advocated by these "liberal" groups.

An analysis of these scores for the decade of the 1970s (see chapter appendix) suggests three conclusions. First, a conservative or a liberal roll-call record comes close to being necessary for gaining the appropriate minor party endorsement. Only 6 of the 357 legislative scores above 50 percent were recorded by legislators who then went on to receive Conservative endorsement for re-election, and only 20 of the 469 scores below that level were recorded by legislators who then received Liberal party support. Second, Conservative and Liberal party endorsements have been concentrated on legislators who have been ideologically the most "pure": Conservative endorsements have been most heavily concentrated on legislators who have recorded scores in the 0–29 percent range, and Liberal endorsements have been most heavily concentrated on legislators in the 70–100 percent range. Finally, it is clear that a conservative or liberal roll-call record is not *sufficient* for gaining minor party endorsement. Sixty-three of the 253 most conservative (0–29) legislative scores were recorded by legislators who subsequently were *not* endorsed in the next election by the Conservative party, and in about half of these instances the candidate was actively opposed by a separate Conservative candidate. Similarly 68 of the 247 most liberal scores (70–100) were recorded by candidates who did *not* subsequently receive the Liberal party endorsement, and again in over half of these instances the candidate was opposed by a Liberal party opponent. Considerations other than ideologies, e.g., patronage, are obviously taken into account when endorsement agreements are negotiated.

The evidence, nevertheless, confirms that the minor parties have, on the whole, lived up to their proclaimed objective of backing legislators of the appropriate ideological leanings. Whether those leanings have been caused by such backing is, however, another question, one which is not answered by the data presented. If there is a linkage between legislative behavior and minor party endorsement, it could take one of three forms. First, conceivably the legislator, having been elected with the help of the major party line on the ballot, could have been recruited from the minor party itself. In fact, however, there have been only a few such instances. The one exception at the Congressional level occurred in 1978 when in return for their agreeing to endorse the Republican statewide ticket, the Conservatives were promised Republican endorsement of a Conservative party member for the desirable First Congressional District.[22] Since 1979, therefore, one of New York's congressmen has been an enrolled Conservative (even though publications such as *Congressional Quarterly* have referred to him as a Republican). At the state legislative level there appear to have been only two or three examples (involving Conservatives) of minor party members winning office as cross-endorsed candidates.[23] (Exact numbers are unavailable since the ballot does not indicate the candidate's party enrollment and since official legislative guides will usually refer to legislators as being either Republican or Democrat, i.e., part of the Republican or Democratic legislative caucus.)

The second possible link between legislative behavior and minor party endorsement is minor party pressure exerted on the major party when it picks its own designees. As explained previously, minor party leaders may threaten to withhold endorsement unless the major party chooses designees of the proper ideological leanings. The consensus among knowledgeable observers is that such threats, explicit or implied, are often successful.

Finally, legislative behavior may be influenced by the implicit threat, used by all pressure groups, that endorsement may be withheld unless the legislator votes "correctly" on the roll call. Again, it is never possible to prove that votes in the legislature are the product of such pressure. Nevertheless, there is frequent speculation in the press that such pressures are at work. Thus Assemblyman Perry Duryea's change of stance on the question of medicaid fundings of abortion was said to be an attempt by him to insure that he received Conservative endorsement for his gubernatorial bid in 1978. (He did.)

## Republican-Democrat Cross-Endorsements

Republican-Democratic joint nominations of candidates for judicial office have been commonplace in New York's electoral politics, extending back to before the turn of the century. While other states struggled over the competing merits of judicial selection by election versus appointment, New York continued with the electoral method, but did so in a way which, its defenders claimed, "took the politics" out of the selection process by making selection a bi-partisan process. Such an eminent jurist as Benjamin Cardozo was first elected to the Court of Appeals in 1917 as the nominee of both the Republican and Democratic parties; and again in 1926 he received the bipartisan nomination for his election to the post of chief justice. Altogether for the first 70 years of this century about two-thirds of all elections to the Court of Appeals featured candidates with Republican-Democratic support. It was only after this system of bipartisanship broke down in the early 1970s and, exacerbating the effect of that change, the challenge primary system of nomination replaced the convention system, that election to the Court of Appeals became deeply enmeshed in hard-fought electoral competition. Largely as a result, reformers were able to achieve their goal of completely removing selection to the Court of Appeals from the electoral process; a 1977 constitutional amendment made these posts subject to gubernatorial appointment.

In contrast to the practice which early evolved for election to the state's highest court, for many years bipartisan backing for Supreme Court judgeships was exceptional. In the period 1921–1930, the first full decade for which complete data are available, only 20 of the 112 Supreme Court vacancies in the state's several judicial districts, or less than 20 percent, were contested by candidates who enjoyed both the Republican and Democratic nominations. The general rule seems to have been that only judges who had served a full 14-year term were entitled to bipartisan support for re-election. There were good reasons for a political party to keep these judicial posts for itself. With their high status, high salary, and long tenure, these posts—as well as other judicial posts at the county and city level—were seen as the ultimate patronage plum, to be distributed only to those within the party who earned them; equally important, Supreme Court judges appointed hundreds of receivers, referees, guardians, and administrators, as well as other court personnel, all of whom could be selected from lists of the party faithful. Despite these incentives—or perhaps because of them—, beginning in the 1930s the proportion of Republican-Democratic cross-endorsements for Supreme Court nominations jumped dramatically to well over 50 percent; bipartisan backing was now given to candidates whether they were incumbents seeking re-election or newcomers to the bench.

Although in decades since the 1930s the proportion of bipartisan nominations has fallen back to nearer 40 percent, such nominations have continued to be a conspicuous part of New York politics. What seems to have precipitated the change was the creation in 1931 of 12 new Supreme Court judgeships in New York's second judicial district. It took a Republican legislature to create the new posts, and a heavily Democratic electorate in New York City to fill them; hence an agreement was worked out whereby each party would benefit. The Republicans would be given five of the new posts for their candidates, and the Democrats would be given seven for theirs; the election would be guaranteed. Despite howls of outrage from good government groups—adding to the controversy was the allegation that nomination to one of these slots carried a price-tag—similar arrangements have explained some of the bipartisan judicial nominations which have been made since that date. Other instances of joint nominations can be explained simply as the mutual desire of the Republican and Democratic county leaders to guarantee "delivery" of a judicial post to their respective worthy candidates. Whatever the motivation, the fact that Supreme Court nominations have been made in judicial conventions, not subject to a primary challenge, has guaranteed that these deals will "stick." Such guarantees have added to the unsavory aroma, including rumors of pricetags, which sometimes surround these conventions.

## Conclusion

New York's system of cross-endorsement has clearly been the product of unforeseen consequences of changes in the state's election law. No one intended that the change to the voting machine and then the enactment of the Wilson-Pakula Law would result in today's multi-party system with its bargaining, leader-to-leader endorsement agreements, and payoffs.

Leaving aside the question of origin and intent, what have been the consequences? Can the system of cross-endorsement be justified? At a time when New York had no direct primaries for statewide offices and when primary contests for lower offices were less frequent than they are today, perhaps it could. The argument could then be made that the system provided a useful means by which the major parties could be forced to be responsive.[24] Today, however, the disadvantages of the system seem clearly to outweigh any possible advantages. First, the system allows the minor parties to wield influence far in excess of their electoral strength. Rather than playing the traditional role of providing warning signals to the major parties, minor parties in New York are able to exert immediate leverage in any district (including the state as a whole) where there is close competition between the two major parties. Political scientists have traditionally thought of two-party competition as desirable because it compels the parties to appeal to a broad spectrum of opinion and, in doing so, to minimize social fragmentation. Demands of various groups are articulated in the legislative and executive halls of government where they can be discussed and compromised by leaders skilled in the art. Under New York's cross-endorsement system, two-party competition leads to the very opposite result: raw demands are fed directly into the ballot box; the major parties are forced to make the concessions before the election; and elections become occasions for divisive rather than healing rhetoric. The Right to Life party, with its signed pledges by the candidates it supports, has most clearly illustrated this result.

A second consequence of the system has been the cynicism it has engendered. No doubt the Liberal party began as a group of dedicated idealists, but today few doubt that its dedication to principle has given way to obsession with patronage. Similarly for the Conservatives; what began as a party which was said to have accepted not a "farthing's" worth of patronage is today described by erstwhile supporters as a party led by "political prostitutes." [25] The way the two major parties negotiate judicial cross-endorsements likewise leads to understandable cynicism with "politics."

A third consequence of the cross-endorsement system is that it has deprived New Yorkers of the major advantage which a multi-party system is said to provide—a wide variety of candidate choices on election day. That advantage has been lost as the minor parties have increasingly come to rely on the major party candidates. Indeed, in the case of Republican-Democratic cross-endorsements, not only for judgeships but for other offices as well—15 congressional or state legislative contests in 1980, the New York City mayorality contest in 1981—even the role of an opposition party has been forfeited; a multi-party system has become a no-party system.

A final consequence of the cross-endorsement system is minority election outcomes. As pointed out in chapter one, such outcomes are common in New York when a minor party enters its own candidate in the general election, sometimes a candidate who has been defeated in a major party primary.

In another environment dual nominations and multiple ballot placement might not have these consequences. In Vermont—one of the other states with a law like New York's—the comparative absence of close competition between Republicans and Democrats would make it difficult for a minor party to play the balance-of-power game. In Connecticut—the other state—a high threshold for official party recognition makes it extremely difficult for a minor party to gain access to the ballot.

The New York legislature could easily amend the election law to establish a similarly high threshold. Or it could eliminate multiple ballot placement. More directly, it could follow the lead of California in 1959 and simply outlaw dual nominations. The chances of the legislature making any of these changes, however, seem remote. Today, well over two-thirds of all legislators have gained their electoral victories with at least some help from the votes received on a minor party line. If there is one thing on which students of legislative behavior are agreed, it is that legislators are extremely reluctant to approve legislation which might jeopardize their re-election prospects.

## Notes

1. In every state except Wisconsin the requirements for obtaining official status are much more formidable than in New York. See *Ballot Access: Vol. 2: A Summary of State Administrative Procedures,* Federal Election Commission (Washington, 1978).

2. See Committee on Rules and Administration, *Election Law Guidebook,* 1978, Table V (Senate Document No. 95–95, 95th Cong. 2nd Session). For some other states, however, it would still be possible for a party's primary write-in vote to result in the selection of a person who was also the official nominee of another party, with the consequence of dual nomination on the November ballot. (For example, in 1973 the mayor of Pittsburgh, through write-in votes, was able to win the nominations of all three official parties—Republican, Democratic, and Constitutional.) Also, in a few states (e.g., Maryland and Pennsylvania) joint nominations are allowed for judicial offices.

3. The twelve parties are, in order: Prohibition (1892–1922), Socialist Labor (1896–1904), Socialist (1900–1938), Independent League (1906–1916), Progressive (1912–1916), American (1914–1916), Farmer Labor (1920–1922), Law Preservation (1930–1934), American Labor (1936–1954), Liberal (1946), Conservative (1962), and Right to Life (1978). The three which initially gained official status through the cross-endorsement method were Independent League, American Labor, and Liberal.

4. Illustrative of the effect of the format change was the fate of the Independent League. In the 1912 gubernatorial election, under the party column ballot format, the party polled approximately 10,000 votes with its endorsement of the Progressive candidate. In 1914, with its voting square occupying the favored position, immedi-

ately to the left of the candidate's (a Democrat) name, the party's vote soared to 125,000. In 1916 its vote dropped to 5,000.

5. The one exception was 1918 when the Prohibition Party endorsed the Republican gubernatorial candidate and thereby polled sufficient votes, 39,000, (the threshold was then 10,000) to retain its official status. Even here, however, the effect of the ballot format could be discerned; in contrast to the 39,000 voters who placed their "X" in the Prohibition party square on the gubernatorial ballot, a full 48,000 voters placed their "X" in the single square which appeared for the separate Prohibition party candidate on the lieutenant governor ballot. After successfully running a separate gubernatorial candidate in 1920, the Prohibition party's separate gubernatorial candidate in 1922 fell below the threshold for official recognition. The Socialist party finally dropped below the official party threshold in 1938. A Law Preservation party, running its own gubernatorial candidate, also gained official recognition in the elections of 1930 and 1932.

6. The one exception was for the office of state Assemblyman, which was used in non-gubernatorial election years to monitor a party's strength for the purpose of determining its eligibility for primary elections.

7. *Matter of Hopper* v. *Britt* (203 N.Y. 144–158, 1911).

8. In the ten-year period preceding the change in the election law, an average of 25 percent of all congressional candidates in Pennsylvania carried the endorsement of a minor party, such as Socialist, Labor, or Prohibition. The California experience is described in James C. Findley, "Cross-Filing and the Progressive Movement in California Politics," *Western Political Quarterly,* Vol. 12 (1959), pp. 699–711; and G.E. Baker and B. Teitelbaum, "An End to Cross-Filing," *National Civic Review,* Vol. 48 (1959), pp. 286–291.

Data relating to Massachusetts and Pennsylvania have been obtained from Congressional Quarterly's *Guide to U.S. Elections* (1975), which is based on data from Michigan's Inter-University Consortium for Political Research. It should be noted, however, that data for New York is sometimes incorrectly reported in this volume, for a reason which is understandable. Because county boards of election did not always follow instructions and report separate party totals in the case of cross-endorsed candidates, the secretary of state, when publishing the figures, sometimes had to report only aggregate results, leading to the impression that the candidate's name appeared on the ballot only once. To use the *Guide*'s own example (p. 544), Emanuel Cellar is shown in 1938 as "D, AM LAB" (Democrat and American Labor), the comma correctly indicating that the name of the candidate appeared at two separate places on the ballot. Yet for the 1934 election, Cellar is shown as "D LP L" (Democrat, Law Preservation, and Liberty), the no-comma format used by the *Guide* to show that the candidate's name appeared only once on the ballot. In fact, the voting-machine ballot format was identical in both elections.

9. J. Daniel Mahoney, *Actions Speak Louder,* Arlington House (New Rochelle, 1968), p. 23. Emphasis mine.

10. Suffolk County Party Chairman as quoted in *Pennysaver News.* July 23, 1980, p. 6.

11. A crucial vote is defined as one where the minor party vote provided the margin of victory or, if the endorsement was not made, *might* have provided the margin of victory. In the latter case, the assumption is made that for statewide office the Liberals will normally endorse the Democratic candidate and the Conser-

vatives the Republican candidate; at the district level, however, any combination is seen as theoretically possible. Thus the Conservative total of crucial district-level votes is composed of 68 instances where the party's cross-endorsement did provide the margin of victory and an additional 176 instances where it might have. The two figures for the Liberals are 32 and 117.

12. The pattern of 1980 congressional and state legislative endorsements was as follows:

| Liberals with | Conservatives with | Right to Life with |
|---|---|---|
| Dem. 105 | Dem.  19 | Dem. 22 |
| Rep.   5 | Rep. 140 | Rep. 70 |

In addition to these 361 endorsements, there were an additional 15 Rep./Dem. endorsements (usually with a minor party as well) and one Democrat endorsed by both Liberal and Conservative parties.

13. See David Butler and Donald Stokes, *Political Change in Britain,* St. Martin's (New York, 1969), p. 326 ff. See also the various polls regarding American voter support for independent candidate John Anderson as reported in the press during the 1980 presidential campaign.

14. For the conspicuous statewide offices, the minor parties have usually polled more votes with separate candidates than with cross-endorsements, but for understandable reasons. Thus when the Liberal party has nominated "name" candidates its vote totals have soared, as when it nominated Franklin D. Roosevelt, Jr., for governor in 1966 (507,000 votes, compared to 263,000 four years later with a Democratic cross-endorsement) and when it nominated, in 1980, Anderson for President and Javits for senator and polled 468,000 and 665,000 votes, respectively (compared with 123,000 for its gubernatorial cross-endorsement in 1978). The largest Conservative vote was polled when James Buckley ran separately in 1970 for U.S. senator and drew 2.2 million votes running against a Republican and a Democrat-Liberal; but six years later, running as a Republican-Conservative, Buckley drew only 311,000 votes on the Conservative line. Also, as long as Rockefeller headed New York's Republican party there was good reason for conservatively inclined voters to vote for separate Conservative gubernatorial candidates; those separate candidates drew more Conservative votes in 1966 and 1970 (510,000 and 423,000) than did the endorsed Republican candidates in 1974 and 1978 (260,000 and 243,000).

15. See Robert Karen, "New York's Satellite Parties: The Politics of Pressure," *The Nation,* Vol. 221, No. 8 (Sept. 20, 1975), p. 236.

16. Evidence of such behavior by major party supporters is found in the fact that in gubernatorial election years a minor party will usually attract more votes on its ballot line for a jointly endorsed Assembly candidate than it will for the jointly endorsed gubernatorial candidate even though, due to normal roll-off, the opposite pattern would be expected. Although generalizing about individual behavior from aggregate data is always dangerous, a reasonable explanation of this vote pattern is that cross-over voters from the major party would prefer to vote for the opposite major party's Assembly candidate by supporting the candidate only, but not the candidate's party.

17. *Matter of Callahan* (200 NY 59, 1910), p. 62. The act declared unconstitutional in this case had been enacted in 1896 and attempted to restrict, but not eliminate, cross-endorsement practices. Despite this decision and the *Hopper* deci-

sion (note 7 above), the Court of Appeals had no difficulty approving the Wilson-Pakula Law (see below) in *Ingersall* v. *Hefferman* (71 NYS 2d, 48, 1947). But then in 1973 the Court found unconstitutional a law which attempted to prevent cross endorsements between an official party and a non-official party. See *Devane* v. *Touhey* (349 N.Y.S. 2d 361).

18. Explaining the difference between the New York and the California experience is the fact that party organization in California was extremely weak. Another factor was that in New York, until the law was changed in 1967, there were no statewide primaries to raid; all nominations were made by party conventions. One of the few examples of a raid occurred in 1926 when a "dry" Republican insurgent won his own party's as well as the Democratic party's primary in New York's 13th Congressional District. Otherwise, in New York Republican-Democratic candidacies have been the outcome of voluntary endorsement agreements for judicial office (see below) or occasionally for other offices.

19. Another amendment to the election law in 1947 brought the cross-endorsement process to full circle: from now on a major party candidate would have to give his explicit permission before a minor party could "authorize" his nomination. Although intended by the Republican legislature to embarrass Democrats who were then being endorsed by the Communist-tinged ALP, today the change carries potentially a more important implication: a major party can now deny the use of its gubernatorial nominee to a minor party seeking to attain or retain official status.

20. Karen, p. 239.

21. In addition to Javits' unsuccessful comeback attempt, Speaker Stanley Steingut, defeated in his Democratic primary in 1978, failed to win re-election to the Assembly in November as the Liberal candidate.

22. The episode illustrated that the major parties, too, can "deliver" on their endorsement agreements; three Republicans tried without success to capture their party's nomination in a hard-fought primary.

23. There are additional Conservative examples at the local government level. On Long Island alone, where Conservative strength is concentrated, there are two counties, 13 towns, and two cities, each with numerous elected positions to fill every other year.

24. The argument is made in Daniel A. Mazmanian, *Third Parties in Presidential Elections,* Brookings Institution (Washington, 1974), pp. 134–35.

25. The early description of the Conservative party is that of William F. Buckley, Jr., "Introduction," in Mahoney, *op. cit.,* p. 11; the later description is taken from the editorial "For Sale to the Highest Bidder," *Suffolk Life,* June 27, 1979, p. 3. The evolution of both the Liberal and Conservative parties provides vivid confirmation of Roberto Michel's theories of organizational evolution and goal-displacement.

**Appendix** NYCLU and ADA Ratings as Predictors of Minor Party Legislative Endorsements, 1972–1978

| Rating Range | STATE ASSEMBLY AND SENATE | | | | CONGRESS | | | |
|---|---|---|---|---|---|---|---|---|
| | 0–29 | 30–49 | 50–69 | 70–100 | 0–29 | 30–49 | 50–69 | 70–100 |
| **Subsequently Endorsed By** | | | | | | | | |
| | REPUBLICAN CANDIDATES | | | | | | | |
| Conservative Party | 164 | 90 | 2 | 0 | 20 | 5 | 0 | 0 |
| Liberal Party | 1 | 1 | 0 | 3 | 0 | 0 | 0 | 3 |
| Neither | 37 | 40 | 5 | 0 | 11 | 10 | 7 | 0 |
| | DEMOCRATIC CANDIDATES | | | | | | | |
| Liberal Party | 6 | 11 | 28 | 122 | 0 | 1 | 4 | 51 |
| Conservative Party | 7 | 13 | 1 | 0 | 0 | 2 | 3 | 0 |
| Neither | 6 | 33 | 53 | 50 | 1 | 10 | 7 | 18 |

Note: The table has been compiled by averaging a legislator's two legislative session scores, then determining whether or not he or she received minor party endorsement at the following election. A legislator who participated in each of the four two-session legislatures preceding the 1972, 1974, 1976, and 1978 elections thus has four rating scores included in the table.

The NYCLU ratings are in terms of the percentage of roll-call votes each session (the number of votes varies from 9 to 20), singled out by the NYCLU, on which a state legislator agrees with the NYCLU position. The ratings are taken from the annual compilations as presented in the organization's publication *N.Y. Civil Liberties*. (For the 1975–76 legislature, data was available for only one session.) ADA ratings for congressmen, also based on percentage agreement, are taken from various editions of *The Almanac of American Politics*.

For the pupose of the table, the assumption is made that all Republican-Conservatives are Republicans endorsed by the Conservative Party, and that all Democratic-Liberals are Democrats endorsed by the Liberal Party. The list of legislators as published in the New York Legislative Record and Index has been used for categorizing as Republican or as Democrat a legislator elected under both those labels, the first-mentioned label being used as the guide; and the same strategy has been used for categorizing as Liberal or Conservative candidates elected under both labels.

# 4.

# Voter Registration
# and Participation
# in New York

THE STORY is told that in the 1840s, when the Croton Reservoir was being constructed, "crowds of thugs" were imported from Philadelphia into New York City on election day to vote for the Tammany candidates. If challenged at the polls, these strangers would claim that they had only recently come to the city as pipe-layers hired to work on the City's new water system. Such stories of election fraud were commonplace in American cities during the latter part of the nineteenth century. Not surprisingly, therefore, it was during this period that the American states first began to enact voter registration laws.[1] New York was among the first to do so, enacting its first registration law in 1859. From then on, in order to cast a ballot on election day a voter would have to have his name on the official voter register, a list prepared several weeks in advance of the election by officially appointed registrars.

## Registration Requirements and Voter Participation

With the other states, New York thus began the struggle with a dilemma which continues to confront all modern democracies: how to balance the conflicting goals of (a) honest elections and (b) maximum voter participation. New York's original 1859 legislation clearly tilted the balance in favor of maximum participation. The law simply instructed the registrars to prepare before each election a list of eligible voters based on the list of participants in the previous election, plus any additional names which, in their judgment, merited inclusion. For the overwhelming proportion of the electorate the law thus imposed no additional burden on the exercise of the franchise. Even those persons whose names did not appear on the previous year's list could have their names added without effort. For example, a known resident could inform the registrar of a new arrival in the neighborhood; or the tax rolls might yield additional names.

*A Dualistic System*

Beginning in the 1860s, however, state policy began to shift away from the goal of maximum participation in favor of more stringent anti-fraud procedures. Most notably, legislation enacted in 1866 stipulated that citizens of New York City and Brooklyn would have to register *each year, in person,* in order to be eligible to vote in the November election. Each October, during a few designated days and specified hours (e.g., 8:00 A.M. to 9:00 P.M.), the usual polling places (e.g., firehouses, schools, churches) would be open for registration. The would-be voter could thus appear, indicate his residence, and, by signature, establish his identity. Only then would his name be included on the official register of voters eligible to participate in the November election. Voting thus became a two-step process, requiring for the citizen twice as much effort, and probably twice the motivation, as before. In 1890 these formidable registration requirements were extended to cover voters in *all* cities, and a few years later they were extended further to cover voters in villages of 5,000 population or more. This burdensome system remained unchanged for over half a century. Not until 1954 was legislation enacted allowing the urban areas to ease the burden of annual, personal registration (see below). By this time, close to 85 percent of the state's citizens resided in the areas covered by the annual, personal registration requirement.

Meanwhile, registration requirements in rural areas remained lenient. Registration was *permanent* in the sense that as long as a person voted each year his name remained on the register; and it was *non-personal* in the sense that someone wishing his or (after 1918) her name added to the register did not have to appear in person before the registrar. The system was defended by rural representatives and Republicans generally on the ground that undue hardship would be placed on rural dwellers if they were required to make two journeys each fall to the nearest polling place; and the system was attacked by Democrats on the ground that it made possible fraudulent "grave yard" voting in staunchly Republican areas. The strength of the defenders' forces was demonstrated at the state constitutional convention of 1894 when they were successful in inserting into the new constitution the provision that no system of personal registration could be imposed on citizens living in areas outside of incorporated cities and villages of 5,000 or more population. Although that clause was removed from the constitution in 1938, not until 1954 did a reluctant Republican legislature finally agree, in a compromise, to allow all counties to impose a personal registration requirement if they wished to do so, and not until 1967 were they required to do so (see below). Helping to force the transition was the fact that by these dates the old standard of population concentrations—incorporated cities and incorporated villages of at least 5,000 population—had been made totally obsolete by suburbanization; thus Long Island's famed Levittown, with its 66,000 population, was treated for registration purposes as simply another "rural" area.

The impact of the two systems of registration—annual-personal versus permanent-non-personal—could clearly be seen in the respective registration rates. As of 1950—the last census year of the dualistic system—for the 28 counties whose populations were in large part covered by the more lenient system, 88 percent of the voting-age population was registered. In sharp contrast, for the remaining dominantly urban counties with the more stringent procedure, the registration rate was only 58 percent. Clearly the lenient procedure yielded a much larger voter register. The question remained, however, whether that difference could be explained as the product of the difference in effort required of the civic-minded citizen living in the two types of areas or, instead, was the product of indolent registrars in the 28 counties failing to purge the voter register of those who had moved from the area or whose names graced the stones in the nearby cemetery. Evidence suggests that the latter explanation accounted for much of the difference. Thus in 1950, in 9 of the 28 counties the number of registered voters actually *exceeded* the number of voting-age citizens found by the census takers that year. In Putnam County for example, the census takers found only 14,000 voting-age citizens; yet the county board of elections reported a total of 22,000 registered voters. Also casting doubt on the validity of the very high 88-percent figure was the fact that in the election of 1950 only 67 percent of the registered voters showed up at the polls whereas in the other counties, with lean registration lists, the proportion was 89 percent. The voting register thus clearly seemed to be less the product of a lenient procedure than it was of the failure of registrars to keep their records current.

The impression must not be left, however, that inaccurate or fraudulent registration was the exclusive province of areas governed by lenient registration procedures. The city of Albany seemed to provide clear evidence to the contrary. With one of the oldest "political machines" in the state, under the direction of Democratic "boss" Daniel O'Connell, Albany was able to boast of astronomical registration rates despite the annual, personal requirement. Thus in 1950 the city reported registration figures which totaled 85 percent of the voting-age population, as determined by the census. This figure contrasted sharply with the more believable figures reported in other cities, such as New York (50 percent), Buffalo (56 percent), and Rochester and Syracuse (58 percent). The charge of "repeaters" (the same person registering several times under different names) seemed all too believable. Unlike in the rural areas, moreover, most of the registrants actually cast ballots on election day—an impressive 98 percent in the 1950 election.

Turning to the other policy goal, viz., maximum voter participation, can we conclude that the more lenient registration system in the 28 counties produced greater levels of voter participation on election day than did the more stringent system? The question cannot easily be answered. Quite apart from the difficulty introduced by fraudulent voting, the major difficulty is that in addition to differences in registration systems there were differences of other kinds between rural and urban areas—e.g., different proportions of various socioeconomic groups—which could also be expected to produce different rates of voter participation in the two types of areas. Accordingly, when we note that in 1950 the 28 counties had a voting-age participation rate of 59 percent whereas in the more restrictive registration counties the voting-age turnout was only 52 percent, there is no way we can be certain that the difference stemmed from differences in the registration systems.

Despite these problems, the argument of reform groups, such as the League of Women Voters, was that voter turnout in New York *was* being depressed by the state's stringent registration requirement for most of its citizens. They found their strongest evidence in the relatively poor turnout rates in New York State compared to the other American states. In the ten presidential elections from 1920 to 1956 the average voter turnout in New York was so low that the state ranked among the bottom third of all the 32 states outside the South or its bordering areas. In its gubernatorial elections New York also ranked toward the bottom of this group.[2] To the reformers it seemed more than coincidental that as of 1954 New York was among only two states in the nation (the other was Texas) to require annual registration of most of its citizens, and it was this argument which helped convince the legislature that year to drop the requirement. Republican and Democratic politicians likewise accepted the common-sense wisdom that annual registration depressed voter participation. Since it was assumed that Democratic voters in urban areas were the ones mainly being discouraged, for this reason, too, the struggle for registration reform assumed strongly partisan overtones.

## *The Change to PPR*

Perhaps the best way to answer the question of the impact of registration procedures on voter turnout is to examine what happened when the system in New York was finally changed as a result of the legislation enacted in 1954. Under that law, the system known as "permanent, personal registration" (PPR) was authorized to be introduced by any county wishing to make use of it. Under PPR, the conscientious citizen would need to register personally once in a lifetime; after that, so long as he or she appeared at the polls at least once in a two-year period (e.g., a voter could skip the odd-year local elections), the name would be retained on the register. The task of the urban voter would be reduced by half. Beginning with four counties in 1956 and New York City, Buffalo, and other urban areas in 1957, the state thus began its transition to a system of voter registration which was easier for the bulk of the citizenry. By the presidential election of 1960 over 90 percent of the electorate had been relieved of the annual registration requirement (or had never been subject to it), and voters who had participated in either the 1958 or the 1959 election could participate with only one trip to the polling station. In 1967 PPR became mandatory for every county in the state. What were the consequences? Did the new system produce the desired effect of increasing voter turnout?

In one sense the objective of the 1954 legislation was realized: registration levels did increase, an average of two percentage points for presidential years and over ten percentage points for both gubernatorial and local election years (see chapter Appendix I). In another sense, however, the result of the change to PPR proved a disappointment; an enlargement of the voter register did not necessarily produce a corresponding increase in voting participation. For presidential elections, there was no increase at all, but actually a slight decrease. Apparently two trips to the polling place in the fall of every fourth year had not had the dampening effect on turnout as the critics had charged. For gubernatorial and local elections, however, the double effort apparently had been a burden; once the burden was halved, not only did the size of the voter register increase, but turnout increased as well, an average of over three percentage points for gubernatorial years and an average of over six points for local election years.

## Continued Reform and Decline

The elimination of the annual registration requirement in 1954 reflected a broad concensus that the major state policy goal should be maximum voter participation and that the danger of voting fraud in the big cities had receded.[3] Just how far the issue of election fraud had dropped from the public agenda was illustrated in 1975 when the legislature amended the election law once more, this time to provide for registration by mail. After over a century of agreement that personal registration was the only sure way to prevent fraud and after years of debate over whether that requirement should be imposed on rural areas, the legislature, with a minimum of discussion, authorized the most casual of methods, mail registration. All a would-be voter had to do now was pick up a registration form at the post office and mail the completed form to the local election board.[4] So successful was this innovation that within a few years over 90 percent of new voters were making use of it.

In little over two decades New York had thus taken two important steps aimed at encouraging voter turnout. Ironically, however, it was precisely during this period that turnout in the state began to reach historic lows (see chapter Appendix II). After 1960 presidential turnout in New York never again reached the levels it had *before* the reforms were introduced, and by the 1970s turnout for gubernatorial and local elections had also fallen to levels below those recorded in the pre-1954 period.[5] Although the declines took place against a backdrop of a nationwide decline in voter participation, the drop-off in New York state was three times the size of the national decline. A study covering the period 1962–1972 found that only three non-Southern or border states (Hawaii, Alaska, Nevada) had an average presidential turnout lower than New York's, and only four (those plus Ohio) had a lower average turnout for gubernatorial elections.[6] The participation decline in New York could be expressed in two ways. First, somewhat fewer registered voters were bothering to vote; in the four presidential elections 1968 through 1980 the respective proportions were 85.8, 79.5, 81.3, and 80.5 percent. More important, however, especially in the 1970s, fewer and fewer persons were bothering to register, or at least to remain registered (Appendix II). To check the latter decline, in 1981 the legislature took still another step toward liberalizing the state's registration requirements. It extended from two years to four years the period within which a voter could remain inactive without having his or her name removed from the register; now it would be possible for a citizen to vote only in the quadrennial presidential contests. After the enactment of PPR registration had followed a consistent four-year cycle: presidential-year highs followed by dramatic drop-offs three years later. With the 1981 law, these cycles would end. Accordingly, it seemed likely that the law might effect turnout in these third-year local elections.[7]

In summary, New York's experience seemed to demonstrate that when citizen interest is sufficiently aroused, the burden of registration is easily overcome; that a lessening of that burden does not translate into a permanently enlarged voter register; and that an enlarged register translates into increased voting mainly for low-stimulus elections. The experience thus confirmed the findings of national opinion surveys, which have shown that the solution to the problem of declining participation lies far less in adjustments in registration laws than it does in arousing voter interest.[8]

That voter interest had declined in New York (and elsewhere) seemed to be related to the fact that the electorate had become less partisan, i.e., less stimulated by strong party organizations and less committed to party loyalty.[9] It is significant that in New York the lowest turnouts have always been recorded in villages, school districts, and fire districts, communities which are "closest to home" but in which the official political parties do not participate. Another pattern is also suggestive: in school district elections many voters will take the trouble of going to the polling station to vote yes or no on the district budget but will fail to vote for candidates running for the school board. This pattern of participation is precisely the opposite from that which prevails at general elections; invariably a state bond issue or constitutional amendment will attract only a fraction of the votes which are cast for the party-sponsored candidates for office. With partisanship and participation related, it is thus not surprising that as the one has declined so has the other.

## The Active Voters: Where? Who? When?

*Where the Voters Are*
The electorate of New York City has never participated in statewide elections to the extent of citizens outside the City. The City's lower turnout for gubernatorial contests was at one time especially noticeable, a pattern which the change to PPR only slightly and temporarily altered. By the late 1960s the discrepancy between City participation rates and rates elsewhere became increasingly noticeable for all statewide contests. The accelerated turnout decline, when combined with the City's population loss, produced a sharp reduction in the City's role in statewide elections: whereas in 1950 the City cast about half of all votes, by 1980 the proportion had fallen to about 30 percent (Table I).

Over the same 30-year period the four suburban counties surrounding New York City doubled their proportion of all votes cast. Yet this proportion of the vote was only slightly higher than the suburbs' portion of the voting-age population, a comparison which seemed to belie the suburbs' reputation as citadels of civic activism. It was in the upstate areas that the voting-age population remained most active; over the 30-year period this region's relative population increased only three percentage points, but its contribution to the total state vote increased twice that much.

The changing geographical distributions of actual voting strength carried potential political implications. Many government benefits, such as school aid and mass-transit aid, are specific to geographical areas. A politically sensitive governor or gubernatorial candidate cannot help but notice where the votes are and where they are not. The implications for Democratic candidates were especially severe. When Averell Harriman won the governorship in 1954, 57 percent of his total vote came from the City; twenty years later the next successful Democratic candidate, Hugh Carey, drew

**Table I.** Percent of Voting-Age Population, and Percent of Total Vote Cast, Three Regions, 1950–1980

|      | New York City | | | Four Suburbs | | | Upstate | | |
|      | Pop. | Vote | Diff. | Pop. | Vote | Diff. | Pop. | Vote | Diff |
|------|------|------|-------|------|------|-------|------|------|------|
| 1950 | 54.7% | 49.4% | −5.3 | 11.0% | 11.9% | +0.9 | 34.4% | 38.6% | +4.2 |
| 1960 | 49.1 | 42.6 | −6.5 | 16.3 | 18.1 | +1.8 | 34.5 | 39.3 | +4.8 |
| 1970 | 46.0 | 38.4 | −7.6 | 19.1 | 22.4 | +3.3 | 34.9 | 39.2 | +4.3 |
| 1980 | 41.2 | 31.7 | −9.5 | 20.9 | 24.2 | +3.3 | 37.9 | 44.2 | +6.3 |

only 40 percent of his vote from the City. Like the Democratic party in the legislature, Democratic governors had come to represent an increasingly heterogeneous constituency.

## Who the Voters Are

The geographical patterns of turnout which have been described have their roots in individual behavioral differences which national surveys have revealed.[10] Of special significance to New York City is the fact that blacks and Hispanics have been found to have extremely low rates of voting participation, and the fact that as of 1980 some 45 percent of the City's population was made up of these minorities. Indeed, so low had minority turnout become by 1970 that the amendment to the Voting Rights Act passed that year— an amendment which brought under the act's provisions any county with voter registration of less than 50 percent—was held to apply to Manhattan, Brooklyn, and the Bronx. Accordingly, the Justice Department had a voice in the reapportionment of congressional districts following the 1970 census (as well as after the 1980 census). The first elections held under the new lines dramatically illustrated the problem of low minority turnout: the total number of persons voting in the four congressional districts with over 50-percent minority population was only 222,000, compared to 485,000 who voted in the four City districts with the least minority population.[11]

Because minorities, as well as persons of low socioeconomic status, are disproportionately represented in the non-voting population and because such persons have also generally been found to be Democratic in their party preference,[12] a reasonable expectation would be that as New York experienced a 15 percentage point decline in registration and voting, the partisan mix of the active electorate would have changed to the detriment of the Democrats. Such a result did not occur. The proportion of enrolled Democrats among the active, registered electorate (including those not enrolled) went from 44 percent in 1956 (the first presidential year when complete statewide figures were available) to 47 percent in 1980. As indicated in chapter one, by other measures, too, Democratic prospects have improved, not declined. Thus whatever damage turnout decline may have inflicted on Democratic prospects for winning statewide contests, that damage appears to have been more than balanced by other factors shaping the partisan disposition of the active electorate.

## When Voters Vote: Core and Peripheral Voters

Turnout figures amply document the fact that voter participation is greatest in presidential elections, less in the "off-year" gubernatorial (as well as congressional and state legislative) contests, and even less in the odd-year local elections. Local elections, in turn, are also subject to periodic surges and declines. When the office of city mayor or county executive is at stake, the turnout is likely to be much higher than in other years. This pattern is clearly reflected in New York City's four-year cycles (Appendix II).

Paralleling the hierarchy of national, state, and local elections is a hierarchy of individual voters: there are some voters who participate in virtually every election, and others who participate only selectively. Said another way, there are "core" voters and "peripheral" voters.[13] A random sample of registered voters in Suffolk

County in 1977 clearly revealed this distinction. Approximately two-thirds of the sample had participated in all or all but one of the elections for which they had been registered.[14] Since the analysis was confined to those persons who had been registered for at least four elections, this meant that these voters had participated in all three types of elections—presidential, gubernatorial, and local. The remaining third of the sample had erratic voting records and included nine percent who voted almost exclusively in the even-year contests. The core voter was more likely to be a committed partisan, enrolled in a party, than an independent: for presidential and gubernatorial elections partisan turnout was five percentage points higher than independent turnout, and for local elections the difference was 14 points. The core voter was also more likely to be a Republican: for local elections Republican turnout was seven percentage points higher than Democratic turnout.[15]

## Conclusion

The following two chapters will be devoted to the subject of reapportionment. As will be seen, during the decade of the 1960s the U. S. Supreme Court held that the "popular will" could find expression in a legislative body only if each of the respective legislative members was elected from districts containing approximately the same number of persons, as determined by the last census. What the Court failed to note, and what surely will be remembered as a great historical irony, was that at the very time it was rendering its decisions, more and more people were failing to vote despite the best efforts of states like New York. Exactly how the "popular will" could be determined when half of the people failed to vote was a question which the Court failed to address.

## Notes

1. The history of registration laws in the United States is found in Joseph P. Harris, *Registration of Voters in the United States,* Brookings Institution (Washington, D.C., 1929).

2. Lester W. Milbrath, "Political Participation in the States," in Herbert Jacob and Kenneth N. Vines, eds., *Politics in the American States,* Little, Brown (Boston, 1965), pp. 38–40.

3. It may be noted, however, that by the mid-1970s Albany's registration rate still remained at a suspiciously high level (75 percent).

4. A form of mail registration had been introduced in 1960. In that year the election law was amended to allow a person who had not voted for two years and who had received notification of the cancellation of registration to sign and return a card indicating that he wished to have the registration validated for another two years.

5. Changes in voter qualifications also affected turnout during this period. Changes which should have served to increase turnout were the elimination of the language requirement in 1965 and in 1970 the reduction of the residency requirement from 90 days to 30 days. On the other hand, 18-year olds became eligible to vote in New York beginning in 1971, and these younger citizens have been shown to participate less than older citizens. Beginning in 1972, the 18-year old franchise was nationwide.

6. Austin Ranney, "Parties in State Politics," in Herbert Jacob and Kenneth N. Vines, eds., *Politics in the American States,* 3rd edition, Little, Brown (Boston, 1976), p. 54.

7. As of 1981 there were 14 states, including New York, which required at least biennial voting participation. The other states had more liberal registration policies, including neighboring Connecticut, where registration lasts a lifetime.

8. See Charles E. Johnson, Jr., *Nonvoting Americans,* U.S. Department of Commerce, Bureau of the Census (Washington, D.C., 1980) in which it is estimated that turnout in the 1976 presidential election would have increased by only about two percentage points had registration laws been eased. Another analysis which considered the effects of registration laws is Raymond E. Wolfinger and Steven J. Rosenstone, *Who Votes?,* Yale University Press (New Haven, 1980).

9. Survey research has shown the positive relationship between electoral participation and partisan commitment. See Angus Campbell, et al., *The American Voter,* University of Chicago Press (Chicago, 1976), pp. 96–7.

10. See Johnson, op. cit.

11. Following the 1980 census Justice Department approval was required not only for the newly-drawn congressional districts but also for the City councilman districts and state legislative districts.

12. See, for example, the results of a New York voter survey in David M. Kovenock, James W. Prothro, and Associates, *Explaining The Vote.* Institute for Research in Social Science (Chapel Hill, North Carolina, 1973), pp. 11–45.

13. The distinction is made by Angus Campbell, "Surge and Decline: A Study of Electoral Change," in Angus Campbell, et al., eds., *Elections and the Political Order,* John Wiley (New York, 1966), pp. 42–3.

14. The analysis focused only on the eight elections held during the period 1970–1977.

15. The partisan turnout percentages were 94.8 percent for presidential, 89.8 percent for gubernatorial, and 74.4 percent for local. The comparable percentages for independents were 90.1, 85.2, and 60.5 percent. The Republican turnout for local elections was 77.4 percent, while the Democratic turnout was 70.0 percent. All differences are accurate to within ±3 percent and significant at the .01 level. The total sample was 990 voters.

**Appendix I.** Registration and Voting Participation Before and After the Introduction of PPR

| | Presidential | | | Gubernatorial | | | Local | | |
|---|---|---|---|---|---|---|---|---|---|
| | % Voting-age Regis. | % Voting-age Vote | % Regis. Vote | % Voting-age Regis. | % Voting-age Vote | % Regis. Vote | % Voting-age Regis. | % Voting-age Vote | % Regis. Vote |
| 1952 | 74.8 | 68.9 | 92.0 | | | | | | |
| 1953* | | | | | | | 58.4 | 44.7 | 76.5 |
| 1954 | | | | 58.0 | 48.9 | 84.2 | | | |
| 1955 | | | | | | | 51.0 | 38.9 | 79.1 |
| 1956 | 71.2 | 66.3 | 93.2 | | | | | | |
| 1957* | | | | | | | 59.4 | 48.0 | 80.9 |
| 1958 | | | | 62.0 | 53.2 | 85.7 | | | |
| 1959 | | | | | | | 62.7 | 44.1 | 70.3 |
| 1960 | 75.1 | 67.3 | 89.7 | | | | | | |
| 1961* | | | | | | | 69.3 | 51.7 | 74.7 |
| 1962 | | | | 68.1 | 52.6 | 77.3 | | | |
| 1963 | | | | | | | 65.0 | 44.9 | 69.1 |
| 1964 | 76.3 | 66.1 | 86.7 | | | | | | |
| 1965* | | | | | | | 73.7 | 54.8 | 74.4 |
| 1966 | | | | 72.6 | 55.1 | 75.9 | | | |
| 1967 | | | | | | | 68.1 | 50.3 | 73.9 |

*Mayoralty election in New York City

**Appendix II.** Percent of Voting-Age Population Registered and Percent Voting in Presidential, Gubernatorial, and Local Elections: New York State, 1950–1980

| | Presidential | | | Gubernatorial | | | Local | | | Registration |
|---|---|---|---|---|---|---|---|---|---|---|
| | State | NYC | Outside NYC | State | NYC | Outside NYC | State | NYC | Outside NYC | State |
| 1950 | | | | 52.8 | 47.7 | 58.8 | | | | 62.0 |
| 1951 | | | | | | | 39.7 | 31.2 | 49.5 | 52.5 |
| 1952 | 68.9* | 64.0 | 74.0 | | | | | | | 74.8 (Presidential) |
| 1953 | | | | | | | 44.7 | 42.1 | 47.3 | 58.4 |
| 1954 | | | | 48.9 | 43.0 | 54.8 | | | | 58.0 |
| 1955 | | | | | | | 38.9 | 27.6 | 49.8 | 51.0 |
| 1956 | 66.3* | 60.7 | 72.3 | | | | | | | 71.2 (Presidential) |
| 1957 | | | | | | | 48.0 | 42.6 | 53.0 | 59.4 |
| 1958 | | | | 53.2 | 45.7 | 59.9 | | | | 62.0 |
| 1959 | | | | | | | 44.1 | 34.7 | 53.2 | 62.7 |
| 1960 | 67.3* | 61.7 | 72.2 | | | | | | | 75.1 (Presidential) |
| 1961 | | | | | | | 51.7 | 48.3 | 54.7 | 69.3 |
| 1962 | | | | 52.6 | 48.0 | 56.6 | | | | 68.1 |
| 1963 | | | | | | | 44.9 | 34.6 | 53.6 | 65.0 |
| 1964 | 66.1* | 60.4 | 71.0 | | | | | | | 76.3 (Presidential) |
| 1965 | | | | | | | 54.8 | 51.8 | 57.4 | 73.7 |
| 1966 | | | | 55.1 | 49.3 | 60.1 | | | | 72.6 |
| 1967 | | | | | | | 50.3 | 38.3 | 60.6 | 68.1 |

| Year | | | | | | | |
|------|------|------|------|------|------|------|------|
| 1968 | 61.4 | 52.2 | 69.3 | 50.2 | 46.7 | 53.2 | 71.5 (Presidential) |
| 1969 | | | | | | | 69.2 |
| 1970 | 53.3 | 42.1 | 60.8 | 41.5 | 27.2 | 53.5 | 68.7 |
| 1971 | | | | | | | 64.4 |
| 1972 | 57.8* | 46.3 | 67.7 | 40.7 | 31.4 | 48.4 | 72.7 (Presidential) |
| 1973 | | | | | | | 70.1 |
| 1974 | 43.6 | 32.2 | 52.9 | 34.8 | 17.9 | 48.1 | 65.7 |
| 1975 | | | | | | | 60.4 |
| 1976 | 51.8* | 39.3 | 61.4 | 36.6 | 27.8 | 42.8 | 63.7 (Presidential) |
| 1977 | | | | | | | 60.8 |
| 1978 | 38.3 | 28.9 | 44.8 | 29.8 | 14.4 | 40.0 | 60.2 |
| 1979 | | | | | | | 56.0 |
| 1980 | 49.4* | 37.9 | 57.5 | | | | 61.2 (Presidential) |

*The national voting-age turnout was: 1952: 61.6; 1956: 59.3; 1960: 63.1; 1964: 61.8; 1968: 60.7; 1972: 55.4; 1976: 54.4; 1980: 53.2.

Methodological Note to Appendix I and II

The total number of active voters each year is based on the so-called "whole number," i.e., the actual number of persons who cast ballots, whether or not they were valid ballots and whether or not the ballots were cast for the most conspicuous office, such as president. Thus measured, turnout shown here is always about one percentage point higher than that shown in analyses which use as the numerator the total valid vote for president or governor. Thus, whereas the Census Bureau shows New York's presidential turnout in 1972 as 56.5 percent, it is shown here as 57.8 percent.

Voting-age population figures for the state are derived from the decennial census, and for non-census, even-numbered years from the estimates issued by the Census Bureau in its population estimate Series P-25. Estimates for odd-numbered years are the mid-points. Estimates for New York and other cities in non-census years are derived from estimates of total population distributions issued periodically by the New York State Department of Health in its publication *Vital Statistics Review*.

Apart from the fact that voting-population figures for non-census years are mere estimates, it also must be pointed out that voting-age population includes some persons who are ineligible to register and vote. The most numerous are aliens. For example, if aliens are taken into account, in 1976 New York's voting-age turnout would be 54.3 percent, not 51.8 percent as shown in Appendix II.

# 5.

# The Impact
# of Reapportionment
# in New York State *

I N 1962 the United States Supreme Court affirmed in *Baker* v.
*Carr*[1] that judicial redress could be sought to compel a state to
reapportion its legislature. Two years later the Court applied the
"one man, one vote" standard to both congressional districts (*Wes-
berry* v. *Sanders*[2]) and state legislative districts (*Reynolds* v. *Sims*[3]),
and in 1968 applied the standard to local governments as well (*Av-
ery* v. *Midland County*[4]). In all these cases the Court asserted that
the equal protection clause of the Fourteenth Amendment required
that legislative districts be as nearly equal in population as prac-
tically possible. In this chapter we shall examine the impact of these
decisions on New York's apportionment of state legislative and
congressional districts. Consideration of local government apportionment will be discussed in chapter six.

## Apportionment Before "Reynolds" and "Wesberry"

*Legislative Apportionment*
By 1960 the New York state legislature was by no means the most
malapportioned legislature in the nation. Of the 15 states (includ-

* Portions of this chapter appeared in REPRESENTATION AND REDISTRICT-
ING ISSUES edited by Bernard Grofman, Arend Lijphart, Robert B. McKay, and
Howard A. Scarrow (Lexington, Mass.: D. C. Heath and Company, Lexington Books,
Copyright, 1982, D. C. Heath and Company). Reprinted by permission of the pub-
lisher.

ing New York) whose apportionment schemes were examined by the Supreme Court at the time of the *Reynolds* decision, 13 had an upper house where the population disparities among districts were more severe than those in New York's Senate; and among the lower houses there were seven with district population discrepancies more severe than those in New York's Assembly.[5] Nevertheless, the New York legislature had for years been cited by political scientists, such as V. O. Key, Jr., as one of the classic examples of malapportionment. One reason was that in New York malapportionment did not stem, as in other states, simply from the legislature's failure to reapportion itself periodically as population growth required; indeed, a constitutional amendment adopted in 1931 insured that the legislature *would* be reapportioned after every decennial census.[6] Rather, in New York malapportionment stemmed from a complex apportionment formula which had been written into the state's constitution in 1894 by delegates who believed that "the average citizen in the rural district is superior in intelligence, superior in morality, superior in self-government, to the average citizen in the great cities."[7] Reflecting this outlook, the 1894 formula made New York's 62 counties the basic unit of legislative representation and awarded representatives to them on a basis which only minimally considered the size of their populations.[8] That this formula produced an enormous discrepancy in the number of citizens each legislator in Albany represented can be seen by looking at what the ratio of representation would have been after the 1960 census had the Court not prevented the implemention of the 1894 formula. There would have been one Assembly district, Schuyler County, containing a population of 14,974, and another district, located in Suffolk County, containing a population of 216,704, over 14 times as large. In the Senate, the district sizes would have ranged from 162,840—a district comprising Putnam and Rockland Counties—to 425,267 or nearly three times as large, in a district located in Nassau County.[9]

To appreciate fully the impact of the *Reynolds* decision these discrepancies must be translated into the arithmetic used by the Supreme Court in determining the constitutionality of a state's legislative apportionment scheme. By the Court's standard, New York's "ideal" district size for its Assembly was the total state population (16,782,304) divided by 150, or 111,882 persons. The Schuyler County district would thus have been 96,908 persons, or

86.6 percent too small, and the district located in Suffolk would have been 104,822 persons, or 93.7 percent, too large. The total discrepancy would thus have been a total of 180.3 percentage points. The comparable statistic for the Senate was 93.8 percentage points. By the time New York came in compliance with the *Reynolds* decision in 1966, the discrepancy range for both houses was under five percentage points and, thus, well within the Court's guidelines, which were finally established at about 15 points.

*Congressional Apportionment*
In contrast to the state's legislative districts, its congressional districts were not subject to a constitutional formula. Nevertheless, when the legislature designed these districts and periodically adjusted them as the state's congressional delegation changed in size, no attempt was ever made to strive for numerical equality of population. Consequently, no less than in the state Assembly and Senate, for congressional districts, too, there were wide discrepancies in the numbers of citizens represented by each of the state's congressmen in Washington. Thus after the 1960 census and before the Court interfered, these districts ranged in size from 348,940 (in Brooklyn) to 469,908 (in the Bronx); in the language of the Court, the discrepancy from the "ideal" amounted to 29.6 percentage points. When, after two tries, by 1970 the state finally came into full compliance with the Court's equal population standards—established by the Court at about one percentage point—every district had a population of almost exactly 409,000.

## The Impact of Reapportionment

In applying the "one man, one vote" principle during the 1960s the Court concentrated its energies almost exclusively on elucidating the exact degree of population equality which it would require, respectively, for congressional, state legislative, and local government districts. Conspicuous by its absence, however, was an acknowledgment by the Court that the most important questions of legislative representation were only *indirectly* related to the numerical equality of district populations. These were the questions of regional representation and political party representation.

*Regional Representation*

Although the 1894 apportionment formula had been devised as a means of depriving city dwellers—especially those in New York City—of equitable representation, by the time of *Reynolds* suburbanites were also being severely penalized, as the examples of Suffolk and Nassau Counties cited above amply document. Nevertheless, on the whole it was still the city of New York which would have been most severely disadvantaged had the Supreme Court not intervened to prevent the application of the 1894 formula following the 1960 census. The City gained a full 11 seats in the Assembly from what it otherwise would have been awarded, a full 13 additional seats after the 1970 census, and 9 seats after the 1980 census (chapter Appendix). Its gain in the Senate was also the greatest among all the regions.

For congressional districts, in contrast, malapportionment did not result in inequitable regional representation. The regional distribution of the state's 41 congressional districts was precisely the same before Court-ordered reapportionment took effect in 1968, and after: New York City, 19 districts; the surrounding suburbs, 8 districts; the remainder of the state, 14 districts.

*Political Party Representation*

Governor Al Smith's observation that New York was "constitutionally Republican" identified what was by far the most important aspect of the constitution's formula for the apportionment of the state legislature, viz., that the Republicans gained and the Democrats lost. Without this impact of malapportionment, which applied likewise to congressional districts, the subject of numerical inequalities would not have been of nearly as much interest to political scientists, such as Key, or to the plaintiffs who brought the apportionment cases before the U.S. Supreme Court. This being so, it is important to note that the Court completely ignored in its decisions the partisan dimension of the various apportionment schemes it reviewed.

The simplest way to describe what had been the partisan consequences of malapportionment in New York is to observe that the less-populated, over-represented rural districts elected nearly all Republicans while the under-represented, more populated urban districts were heavily Democratic in their preferences. Accord-

ingly, over the years the partisan complexion of the New York legislature and the New York congressional delegation was much more
heavily Republican than it would have been had legislative and
congressional districts been of equal population. Some idea of how
much different can be seen from analysis of the results of the first
Assembly election held in 1966 under the Court-ordered equal population districts. In that year the Democrats elected 80 members
of the Assembly and the Republicans 70. By extrapolation it can
be estimated that had the 1894 formula prevailed the distribution
would have been precisely the reverse, the Republicans winning 80
seats and the Democrats 70. Analysis of the subsequent seven elections (1968–80) likewise indicates that in each case there would
have been a difference in outcome of approximately ten seats had
the old formula prevailed. Because New York's two major parties
have always formed disciplined blocs in the legislature, a ten-seat
difference can easily determine which of the parties will be in the
majority and hence in control of legislative policy. From 1920 until
the Democratic landslide of 1964, New York Democrats had won
majority control of the Assembly only once, in 1934. From 1966
through 1980, in contrast, the Democrats won control of the Assembly in five of the eight elections. At least three of these results—1966, 1978 and 1980—could be traced directly to the with-
drawal of the 1894 formula, and it seemed likely that the other
Democratic majority outcomes could, at least in part, be traced indirectly to that change since incumbents are usually favored to win
re-election.

The Democrats made gains in the state Senate also, as well as
in congressional representation, once equal population districts were
introduced. However, the complexity of the old Senate apportionment formula and the fact that there never had been a formula for
congressional apportionment make it impractical to attempt to estimate the size of these gains.[10]


*Seat-Vote Ratios*
Seat-vote ratios, which are expressions of how a party's share of
the statewide vote compares with its share of seats won, provide
the most convenient method of measuring the partisan impact of
former malapportionment and the change to equal population districts. The plaintiffs who challenged New York's apportionment

**Table I.** Proportionality of Seats and Votes: Democratic Proportion of two Party[a] Vote and Seats Won, New York State Congressional, Senate and Assembly Elections, Before and After Reapportionment

| | Congress | | | Senate | | | Assembly | | |
|---|---|---|---|---|---|---|---|---|---|
| | % Vote | % Seats | Diff. | % Vote | % Seats | Diff. | % Vote | % Seats | Diff. |
| 1952 | 43.5 | 32.6 | −10.9 | 41.9 | 32.1 | − 9.8 | 42.8 | 30.7 | −12.1 |
| 1954 | 47.1 | 39.5 | − 7.6 | 47.5 | 39.7 | − 7.8 | 47.8 | 39.3 | − 8.5 |
| 1956 | 43.2 | 37.2 | − 6.0 | 43.0 | 27.6 | −15.4 | 43.5 | 32.0 | −11.5 |
| 1958 | 48.3 | 41.9 | − 6.4 | 48.0 | 37.9 | −10.1 | 48.0 | 38.0 | −10.0 |
| 1960 | 50.7 | 46.5 | − 4.2 | 50.3 | 43.1 | − 7.2 | 50.7 | 43.3 | − 7.4 |
| 1962 | 49.3 | 46.3 | − 3.0 | 48.4 | 41.4 | − 7.0 | 48.8 | 41.3 | − 7.5 |
| 1964 | 58.0 | 61.0 | + 3.0 | 57.7 | 53.5 | − 4.2 | 57.6 | 58.0 | + 0.4 |
| | | | | | Average | − 8.8 | | Average | − 8.2 |
| | | | | | Reapportionment | | | | |
| 1966 | 51.7 | 58.5 | + 6.8 | 49.5 | 45.6 | − 3.9 | 51.0 | 54.7 | + 3.6 |
| | Average | − 3.5 | | | | | | | |
| | Reapportionment | | | | | | | | |
| 1968 | 51.9 | 61.0 | + 9.1 | 45.9 | 45.6 | − 0.3 | 49.5 | 54.0 | + 4.5 |
| 1970 | 52.2 | 63.4 | +11.2 | 48.2 | 45.6 | − 2.6 | 49.5 | 49.3 | − 0.2 |
| 1972 | 51.0 | 53.9 | + 2.9 | 47.5 | 43.3 | − 4.2 | 49.6 | 46.7 | − 2.9 |
| 1974 | 58.2 | 69.2 | +11.0 | 53.5 | 48.3 | − 5.2 | 56.3 | 61.3 | + 5.0 |
| 1976 | 58.6 | 69.2 | +10.6 | 50.6 | 46.7 | − 3.9 | 56.3 | 63.3 | + 7.0 |
| 1978 | 55.1 | 66.7 | +11.6 | 48.2 | 50.0 | + 1.8 | 52.5 | 60.7 | + 8.2 |
| 1980 | 51.4 | 59.0 | + 7.6 | 46.8 | 46.7 | − 0.1 | 51.6 | 58.7 | + 7.1 |
| | Average | + 9.1 | | | Average | − 2.1 | | Average | + 4.1 |

[a] See footnote 11.

schemes were fully aware that the Republican proportion of state legislative and congressional seats had usually been substantially higher than the Republican proportion of the statewide vote. The extent of the Republican advantage under malapportionment is shown at the top half of Table I, and the change after Court-ordered reapportionment is reflected in the figures at the bottom half of the table.[11] It will be seen that in the Assembly there were once heavily pro-Republican disproportionalities, but that today the disproportionalities are more likely to be pro-Democratic. For the Senate, there were also once heavily pro-Republican disproportionalities, but these, too, have been eliminated; the disproportionalities today are of modest size. For the state's congressional representation, pro-Republican disproportionalities used to be the rule; today there are pro-Democratic disproportionalities of even greater size. Clearly, the Court's "one man, one vote" mandate had a dramatic impact on seat-vote ratios, the Court's refusal to consider them notwithstanding.

## Fairness of Apportionment and Districting

Seat-vote ratios provide more than a convenient measure of the partisan impact of former malapportionment compared to today's equal apportionment; just as important, seat-vote ratios provide a normative standard, grounded in democratic theory, by which the *fairness* of an apportionment scheme may be judged. The U.S. Supreme Court came unwittingly close to legitimizing the partisan seat-vote mode of evaluation when it cited the fact that if New York's 1894 formula were allowed to govern the reapportionment of the Assembly following the 1960 census, a mere 37.5 percent of the state population, living in the 76 least populous Assembly districts, would be able to control a majority of the Assembly. The Court found this outcome incompatible with democratic principles implicit in the Fourteenth Amendment. Specifically, the Court observed that in all states "Since legislatures are responsible for enacting laws by which all citizens are to be governed, they should be bodies which are collectively responsive to the popular will." [12] The Court thus acknowledged that a scheme of representation should be evaluated in terms of its *collective* impact, not in terms of separate outcomes in individual districts.

This statewide, collective perspective is precisely the one held by those who would judge the fairness of an apportionment-districting scheme by the standard of partisan seat-vote ratios. Now, however, that perspective is applied to the state's actual voters, not to the state's total population; and the collectivity which is identified as reflecting the "popular will" is the total number of voters in the state who vote for candidates of one party, not the total number of citizens who make up a majority of the population. The perspective is derived from the model of party government: voters vote for a party, not for a candidate; and they do so for reasons associated with the party's statewide policy positions, or because they want to reward or punish a statewide party for its previous record, such as the performance of its gubernatorial incumbent or its legislative majority. From the party-government perspective, therefore, a fair apportionment-districting scheme is one which accurately translates the aggregate of these party preferences into each party's fair share of legislative seats. Especially repugnant is a disproportionality which is such that a minority of voters, through their party, are able to exercise majority legislative control, with all the policymaking power that implies. Such an outcome had occurred in New York in the elections of 1932, 1936, 1940, and 1960 when in each of those years a minority of Republican votes produced a majority of Republican legislators in both the Assembly and the Senate. It was the kind of outcome which those who challenged New York's apportionment scheme did not want to see occur again.

But such outcomes did occur again, as in 1974 when a minority of Republican votes produced a majority of Senate seats or in other years when seat-vote disproportionalities not only remained, but became larger in size than those of earlier years.

*Distribution, Districting, and Gerrymandering*

The reason that seat-vote disproportionalities did not disappear with the change to equal apportionment is that these ratios are affected by factors other than apportionment, most notably by the way a party's supporters are distributed among districts. Supporters may be so heavily *concentrated* in some districts that the party "wastes" its vote in victories won by margins of, say, 90 percent to 10 percent; and/or supporters may be so *dispersed* among many districts that the party "wastes" its vote in contests it loses by margins of, say, 49 percent to 51 percent. In either case the party's share of seats will be much smaller than its share of votes. Although some waste of vote is inevitable due to the natural distribution of party supporters—the concentration of Democratic voters in New York City is an obvious example—other waste is the result of districting and, especially, of gerrymandering, which is districting deliberately designed to waste the vote of one party and maximize the number of seats won by the other.

In the judgment of one of the plaintiffs who challenged New York's apportionment schemes before the Supreme Court, New York State had been the most conspicuous example in the nation of Republican-engineered gerrymandering of congressional districts, a practice which resulted in large anti-Democratic seat-vote disproportionalities. Accordingly, he urged the Court to make the practice of gerrymandering illegal.[13] The Court not only ignored his plea, but by insisting on almost exact population equality for congressional and legislative districts—thereby requiring that district lines cut through natural community boundaries—the Court actually increased the opportunities for gerrymandering.

According to observers close to the process, these opportunities were fully realized. The districting which governed elections during the period 1966–1970 was said to be the product of a bipartisan gerrymandering with a Republican Senate and a Democratic Assembly agreeing to enact each other's obviously self-serving maps. In contrast, the districting which governed congressional elections beginning in 1970 and legislative elections beginning in 1972 was described as one-party gerrymandering, designed by an all-Republican legislature and signed by a Republican governor.[14]

*Another Method of Analysis*

To assess the accuracy of these various charges of gerrymandering, as well as to assess more accurately the partisan impact of former malapportionment and the change to equal population districts, it is necessary that we turn to another method of analysis. The problem with the simple seat-vote ratios of the kind shown in Table I is that they may be misleading. We can never expect that a single-member-district plurality system of election will produce an exact proportionality between seats and votes; only a European-style system of proportional representation will do that. At best, all we can expect is a reasonable approximation, and sometimes not even that, since studies have shown that the more a party's vote exceeds 50 percent of the total vote the greater will be its "bonus" of disproportionality in the number of seats it wins. Thus, for example, the fact that in 1952, as shown in Table I, the Republicans won nearly 70 percent of the seats in the Assembly with only 57 percent of the vote did not necessarily indicate that the apportionment-districting system was *biased* in favor of the Republicans; a disproportionality of that magnitude could occur simply as the result of the "bonus" tendency. If that be the case, however, we should expect that the same "bonus" be awarded to the Democrats, if and when they were to win 57 percent of the vote. Needed, then, is a method of analysis which can show whether or not that hypothetical outcome would occur.

Such a method is presented in Table II, which projects what the seat-vote ratios *would have been* if, in each district throughout the state—and thus in the statewide total also—a party had increased its vote by one, two, three, etc. percentage points—the other party's vote thereby decreasing by that amount; or if in each district throughout the state—and thus in the statewide total also—the party had decreased its vote by one, two, or three, etc. percentage points, the other party's vote thereby increasing by that amount.[15] These projections are shown for a large number of election years, not just one, in order that the impact of the apportionment-districting system can be examined in the context of a variety of circumstances. Rather than project seat-vote ratios under all possible outcomes in these various elections, Table II focuses only on the realistic 40–60 percent range, identifying what the Democratic and Republican seat proportions would have been at five selected levels of statewide support: 40 percent (the other party 60 percent), 45 percent (55 percent), 50 percent (50 percent), 55 percent (45 percent) and 60 percent (40 percent).

On the basis of these simulated outcomes we can pose again the question of whether the pre-1966 (for Congress, pre-1968) apportionment-districting system was inherently biased against the Democrats. There is now no question that it was. For all the pre-reapportionment elections, projected results show that the Republicans, at virtually all points in the 40–60 percent range, would win more seats than the Democrats would win with the same proportion of the vote. Thus, to return to our example, the large pro-Republican disproportionalities in the 1952 congressional and legislative elections shown in Table I were not merely the result of the "bonus" effect; had the Democrats polled 57 percent of the statewide vote in that election they would *not* have won some 70 percent of the seats as did the Republicans, but only about 55 percent. In all the pre-reapportionment elections the anti-Democratic bias was especially conspicuous at the crucial level of around 50 percent, so that when the electorate was about evenly split between the two parties, the Republicans could win control of both houses by wide margins; in contrast, the Democrats would have needed to win close to 55 percent of the vote in order to have captured majority control. Even in 1964 when (as shown in Table I) the election resulted in the Democratic portion of Assembly and congressional seats slightly exceeding the party's portion of the vote,

**Table II.** Projected Percentage of Legislative Seats Won by Democrats and Republicans at Selected Percentages of the Statewide, Two-Party[a] Vote, 1964–1980

| Percent of vote[b] | | Assembly | | | | | Senate | | | | |
|---|---|---|---|---|---|---|---|---|---|---|---|
| | | ±40 | ±45 | ±50 | ±55 | ±60 | ±40 | ±45 | ±50 | ±55 | ±60 |
| 1964 | Dem. | 32.7 | 39.3 | 44.7 | 52.0 | 65.3 | 34.5 | 41.4 | 44.8 | 58.6 | 89.7 |
| | Rep. | 34.7 | 48.0 | 55.3 | 60.7 | 67.3 | 10.3 | 41.4 | 55.2 | 58.6 | 65.5 |
| | Bias | − 2.0 | − 8.7 | −10.6 | − 8.7 | − 2.0 | +24.2 | ± 0 | −10.4 | ± 0 | +24.2 |
| 1966 | Dem. | 38.7 | 45.3 | 53.3 | 60.0 | 72.7 | 42.1 | 43.9 | 49.6 | 52.6 | 70.2 |
| | Rep. | 27.3 | 40.0 | 46.7 | 54.7 | 61.3 | 29.8 | 47.4 | 50.4 | 56.1 | 57.9 |
| | Bias | +11.4 | + 5.3 | + 6.6 | + 5.3 | +11.4 | +12.3 | − 3.5 | − 0.8 | − 3.5 | +12.3 |
| 1968 | Dem. | 40.0 | 45.3 | 54.7 | 60.0 | 71.3 | 43.9 | 45.6 | 49.1 | 54.4 | 71.9 |
| | Rep. | 28.7 | 40.0 | 45.3 | 54.7 | 60.0 | 28.1 | 45.6 | 50.9 | 54.4 | 56.1 |
| | Bias | +11.3 | + 5.3 | + 9.4 | + 5.3 | +11.3 | +15.8 | ± 0 | − 1.8 | ± 0 | +15.8 |
| 1970 | Dem. | 40.7 | 44.7 | 49.3 | 59.3 | 72.7 | 42.1 | 45.6 | 50.9 | 56.1 | 63.2 |
| | Rep. | 27.3 | 40.7 | 50.7 | 55.3 | 59.3 | 36.8 | 43.9 | 49.1 | 54.4 | 57.9 |
| | Bias | +13.4 | + 4.0 | − 1.4 | + 4.0 | +13.4 | + 5.3 | +1.7 | +1.8 | +1.7 | +5.3 |
| 1972 | Dem. | 36.7 | 40.0 | 47.3 | 58.7 | 69.3 | 36.7 | 40.0 | 45.0 | 58.3 | 73.3 |
| | Rep. | 30.7 | 41.3 | 52.7 | 60.0 | 63.3 | 26.7 | 41.7 | 55.0 | 60.0 | 63.3 |
| | Bias | + 6.0 | − 1.3 | − 5.4 | − 1.3 | + 6.0 | +10.0 | − 1.7 | −10.0 | − 1.7 | +10.0 |
| 1974 | Dem. | 39.3 | 44.0 | 50.0 | 58.7 | 70.0 | 38.3 | 40.0 | 43.3 | 53.3 | 75.0 |
| | Rep. | 30.0 | 41.3 | 50.0 | 56.0 | 60.7 | 25.0 | 46.7 | 56.7 | 60.0 | 61.7 |
| | Bias | + 9.3 | + 2.7 | ±0 | + 2.7 | + 9.3 | +13.3 | − 6.7 | −13.4 | − 6.7 | +13.3 |
| 1976 | Dem. | 40.7 | 47.3 | 55.3 | 62.7 | 70.0 | 40.6 | 41.1 | 46.1 | 61.1 | 69.4 |
| | Rep. | 30.0 | 37.3 | 44.7 | 52.7 | 59.3 | 30.6 | 38.9 | 53.9 | 58.9 | 59.4 |
| | Bias | +10.7 | +10.0 | +10.6 | +10.0 | +10.7 | +10.0 | + 2.2 | − 7.8 | + 2.2 | +10.0 |
| 1978 | Dem. | 46.0 | 53.3 | 58.7 | 63.3 | 71.3 | 40.0 | 46.7 | 50.0 | 56.7 | 63.3 |
| | Rep. | 28.7 | 36.7 | 41.3 | 46.7 | 54.0 | 36.7 | 43.3 | 50.0 | 53.3 | 60.0 |
| | Bias | +17.3 | +16.6 | +17.4 | +16.6 | +17.3 | + 3.3 | + 3.4 | ± 0 | + 3.4 | + 3.3 |
| 1980 | Dem. | 49.3 | 54.7 | 61.3 | 63.3 | 69.3 | 45.0 | 46.7 | 50.0 | 53.3 | 66.7 |
| | Rep. | 30.7 | 36.7 | 38.7 | 45.3 | 50.7 | 33.3 | 46.7 | 50.0 | 53.3 | 55.0 |
| | Bias | +18.6 | +18.0 | +12.6 | +18.0 | +18.6 | +11.7 | ± 0.0 | ± 0.0 | ± 0.0 | +11.7 |

[a] See footnote 11.

[b] Because the projections have been calculated beginning with the actual Democratic proportion of the statewide vote carried to one decimal place (e.g. 46.4%), the five levels of support shown in the table (40%, 45%, etc.) refer to a slightly higher percentage of Democratic support (e.g. 40.4%, 45.4%, etc.) and a slightly lower percentage of Republican support (e.g. 39.6%, 44.6%, etc.).

this seemingly pro-Democratic bias was misleading; projection shows that had the Democratic vote fallen to 50 percent, or even several points above that, the Republicans would easily have captured the majority of the seats (Table II).

Beginning with the first reapportionment elections, the pattern of bias changed dramatically. As shown in Table II, for the three state legislative elections held under equal population districts and alleged bipartisan gerrymandering (1966–1970), the pattern of bias was either heavily in favor of the Democrats, as in the Assembly, or the bias was virtually eliminated, as in the Senate. Beginning in 1972, however, a quite different pattern of bias emerged, one which confirms the charge that the post-1970 districting was the product of Republican-designed gerrymandering. As will be seen, the anti-Democratic bias appears again, especially in the Senate; Democrats now have to poll considerably more votes than the Republicans in order to win the same number of seats. The most startling story told by the projections, however, is that they indicate that after 1972 the Republican gerrymandering was no longer effective; changing voting patterns completely undid the careful work of the Republican cartographers. By 1974 the Assembly districting scheme had become virtually completely unbiased, and beginning in 1976 it turned against the party which designed it. If, in these and later years, the Republicans had managed to win a majority of the statewide vote, they would *not* have been able to win a majority of the Assembly seats. In the Senate, too, the effect of gerrymandering wore off as the decade progressed, with the bias turning against the Republicans by the time of the 1980 election; Republicans retained control of this house despite of, not because of, the districting scheme.[16]

Following the 1980 census the two major parties followed the example they had established in the 1960s: a Democratic Assembly and a Republican Senate agreed to a mutually acceptable gerrymandering. The results of the 1982 election—the continuation of a split legislature—demonstrated the artful work of the cartographers. Projections show that had the Democrats won a majority of the votes cast for the state Senate candidates they still would have fallen far short of winning a majority of the Senate seats; and had the Republicans won a majority of the Assembly vote they, too, would have fallen far short of majority control. The lesson from the 1970s, however, was that the partisan bias built into the election map would probably be short lived.

*Conclusion*

After the legislature drew its post-1980 district lines these were carefully scrutinized, both by the U.S. Justice Department and by a Federal district court, to make sure that two groups within the New York electorate, blacks and Hispanics, would be able to elect legislators in numbers which bore a resemblance to each groups' proportion of the population. Such attempts at "affirmative gerrymandering" not only raised the question of whether or not this type of gerrymandering would be any more successful than old-style partisan gerrymandering, but also raised the more fundamental question of why the two most important groups in the state, Republican voters and Democratic voters, should not also be proportionately represented in the legislature. This was the kind of basic, searching question concerning the nature of democratic representation which the courts had not yet begun to address.

## Notes

1. 369 U.S. 186.

2. 376 U.S. 1.

3. 377 U.S. 533; decided at the same time was New York's own reapportionment case *WMCA* v. *Lomenzo,* 377 U.S. 633.

4. 390 U.S. 533.

5. Robert Dixon, *Democratic Representation,* Oxford University Press (New York, 1968), p. 266.

6. Prior to this amendment the legislature had been reapportioned twice during the century, in 1907 and 1917. The next reapportionment followed the 1940 census.

7. *Revised Record of the Constitutional Convention of 1894,* Vol. IV, p. 10.

8. A good description of these formulas will be found in Gus Tyler and David I. Wells, "New York: Constitutionally Republican," in Malcolm Jewell, ed., *The Politics of Reapportionment,* Atherton Press (New York, 1962), pp. 232–239. Parts of that formula, such as provisions governing the size of the Senate, are still in effect since they can be reconciled with the equal population requirement. Also still in effect are the constitutional provisions stipulating that district lines shall not cut through towns or city blocks.

9. Figures are those found in *WMCA* v. *Lomenzo,* 208 F. Supp. 368 (1962) and 377 U.S. 633 (1964). Since under the old system district lines within counties were drawn by the counties themselves, these figures are necessarily estimates of what the district sizes would have been.

10. The Senate had been less malapportioned than the Assembly. Hence it had been controlled by the Democrats in six consecutive yearly elections during 1932–1937, in contrast to only one Democratic majority in the Assembly.

11. Because of New York's cross-endorsement system, there is no completely satisfactory way to calculate partisan vote and seat totals. Seat percentages are

especially sensitive to the vagaries of minor party strategies of giving or withholding endorsement of major party candidates. For the purposes of Table I and Table II, therefore, only the two-party vote is considered, and a district is considered as "won" by one of the two major parties if that party's vote exceeds the vote of the other major party. To allow comparison with the actual election outcomes, the following are the vote and seat percentages, based on the total vote received by the two major party candidates, including votes received on other lines of the ballot. (The vote received by separate minor party candidates is ignored when making the vote calculations.) As in Table I the percentages are expressed in terms of Democratic totals, the Republican percentages being the reciprocals of these. For most of these figures the author is indebted to David Wells.

|      | Congress | | | Senate | | | Assembly | | |
|------|------|-------|-------|------|-------|-------|------|-------|-------|
|      | Vote | Seats | Diff. | Vote | Seats | Diff. | Vote | Seats | Diff. |
| 1952 | 45.8 | 37.2 | − 8.6 | 43.2 | 33.9 | − 9.3 | 43.9 | 34.7 | − 9.2 |
| 1954 | 49.3 | 39.5 | − 9.8 | 49.2 | 41.4 | − 7.8 | 48.4 | 40.0 | − 8.4 |
| 1956 | 45.1 | 39.5 | − 5.6 | 44.9 | 34.5 | −10.4 | 44.5 | 36.0 | − 8.5 |
| 1958 | 50.7 | 44.2 | − 6.5 | 50.3 | 41.4 | − 8.9 | 50.2 | 38.7 | −11.5 |
| 1960 | 52.6 | 51.2 | − 1.4 | 51.1 | 43.1 | − 8.0 | 51.8 | 44.0 | − 7.8 |
| 1962 | 50.8 | 48.8 | − 2.0 | 50.1 | 43.1 | − 7.0 | 50.2 | 43.3 | − 6.9 |
| 1964 | 58.4 | 65.9 | + 7.5 | 58.7 | 56.9 | − 1.8 | 58.4 | 58.7 | + 0.3 |
| 1966 | 52.1 | 63.4 | +11.3 | 50.7 | 45.6 | − 5.1 | 51.9 | 53.3 | + 1.4 |
| 1968 | 51.4 | 63.4 | +12.0 | 46.2 | 42.1 | − 4.1 | 48.9 | 48.0 | − 0.9 |
| 1970 | 51.3 | 58.5 | + 7.2 | 47.0 | 43.9 | − 3.1 | 46.5 | 47.3 | + 0.8 |
| 1972 | 50.4 | 56.4 | + 6.0 | 46.6 | 38.3 | − 8.3 | 48.3 | 44.7 | − 3.6 |
| 1974 | 57.5 | 69.2 | +11.7 | 51.3 | 43.3 | − 8.0 | 54.8 | 58.7 | + 3.9 |
| 1976 | 58.0 | 71.8 | +13.8 | 48.8 | 41.7 | − 7.1 | 55.7 | 60.0 | + 4.3 |
| 1978 | 48.4 | 69.2 | +10.8 | 47.3 | 41.7 | − 5.6 | 51.4 | 57.3 | + 5.9 |
| 1980 | 49.4 | 56.4 | + 7.0 | 44.6 | 41.7 | − 2.9 | 49.4 | 56.7 | + 7.3 |

12. 377 U.S., 565.

13. *Wells* v. *Rockefeller,* 394 U.S. (1969). Wells' description of congressional gerrymandering is to be found in his chapter on "New York: Constitutionally Republican," op. cit.

14. A good account of these gerrymanderings is David I. Wells, "It's Just a Question of Slicing the Salami," *Empire State Report,* Vol. 4, No. 5 (1978), pp. 9–13.

15. This methodology was first suggested by David Butler in his Appendix to H.G. Nicholas, *The British General Election of 1950,* Macmillan (London, 1951), pp. 306–333. Edward R. Tufte applied the method to American election data in "The Relationship Between Seats and Votes in Two-Party Systems," *American Political Science Review,* Vol. 68 (1974), pp. 540–554.

16. Mayhew has argued that gerrymandering often fails to achieve its objective because the partisans in charge spread their support too thinly across the legislative map, trying to win as many districts as possible. See David R. Mayhew, "Congressional Representation: Theory and Practice in Drawing the Districts," in Nelson Polsby, ed, *Reapportionment in the 1970s,* University of California Press (Berkeley, 1971), p. 283.

**Appendix.** Number of Seats in New York State Assembly by Region: The Impact of Reapportionment

| Region | After 1950 Census 1894 Formula | After 1960 Census | | | After 1970 Census | | | After 1980 Census | | |
|---|---|---|---|---|---|---|---|---|---|---|
| | | Protected by 1894 Formula | Actual, Equal Pop. | Diff. | Projected by 1894 Formula | Actual, Equal Pop. | Diff. | Projected by 1884 Formula | Actual, Equal Pop. | Diff. |
| NYC | 65 | 57 | 68 | +11 | 52 | 65 | +13 | 51 | 60 | + 9 |
| Four Suburban Counties[a] | 16 | 22 | 26 | + 4 | 26 | 30 | + 4 | 27 | 33 | + 6 |
| Populous Upstate Counties[b] | 31 | 33 | 34 | + 1 | 34 | 37 | + 3 | 34 | 36 | + 2 |
| Other Upstate Counties | 38 | 38 | 22 | −16 | 38 | 18 | −20 | 38 | 21 | −17 |

[a] Nasau, Suffolk, Rockland, Westchester.
[b] Albany, Broome, Chautauqua, Dutchess, Erie, Monroe, Niagara, Oneida, Onondaga, Orange, Rensselaer, St. Lawrence, Schnectady, Ulster. These are counties that had a population of 100,000 or more in 1960.

# 6.

# Reapportionment in County Government: Competing Systems of Representation and Their Consequences *

IN NEW YORK STATE questions of apportionment have loomed large not only with respect to congressional and state legislative districts, but also with respect to county government. There are two reasons for this. First, county government in New York has been entrusted with heavy responsibilities, such as the provision of welfare services. Reflecting the role played by counties, all local governments in New York account for a higher proportion of the combined state and local expenditure (about 75 percent), and combined state and local revenues (about 55 percent), than do local governments in any other American state. Second, as indicated in earlier chapters, in New York the counties serve as the basic unit of party organization with the parties' county chairmen being among the most influential political actors in the state. These two features of counties in New York have combined to produce a third reality: control of county government and the patronage possibili-

* This chapter was written in part in collaboration with Bernard Grofman. Portions have been taken from Bernard Grofman and Howard Scarrow, "Weighted Voting in New York," *Legislative Studies Quarterly,* Vol. VI (May, 1981), pp. 287–304. Reprinted by permission of the Comparative Legislative Research Center, University of Iowa, copyright © 1981.

ties attendant thereto are prizes highly valued by the political parties.

## Representation Prior to the 1960s

Prior to the U.S. Supreme Court's finding that their system of government was unconstitutional, New York's 57 counties (outside New York City) were governed by boards of supervisors. Under this system, also common to states like New Jersey, Michigan, Illinois, and Wisconsin, each of the supervisors served not only as the town's executive officer but also as the town's representative on the all-county governing board. Where a county included a city within its borders, the city was divided into wards, and each ward also elected a representative—dubbed "supervisor"—to the county board. Thus Buffalo was divided into 27 wards, Rochester into 24, and Syracuse into 19.

It requires little imagination to see the possibilities for malapportionment which were inherent in this scheme of county government. Towns having populations of a few hundred had equal representation with towns and wards having populations in the thousands. Thus, whereas by 1960 the largest state assembly district was 14 times the size of the smallest, by that date the majority of counties presented examples of much more extreme malapportionment. In Suffolk County the largest town was 132 times the size of the smallest; yet both town supervisors sat on the county board with equal voting power. Using one of the measurement used by the U.S. Supreme Court in *Reynolds,* a mere 17 percent of Suffolk's population could, through their six representatives on the ten-member board, determine county policy.

Throughout most of the state's history the supervisor system of county government severely discriminated against the cities. As late as 1930, for example, the city of Buffalo's 27 ward representatives constituted only 46 percent of the board membership even though Buffalo accounted for 75 percent of the Erie County population. By 1960, however, Buffalo as well as other cities had begun to gain close to their proportionate share of representatives; now it was the larger towns which were most severely disadvantaged, towns like Erie's Tonawanda (population 107,000), Suffolk's Islip (278,000), and Westchester's Greenburgh (85,000). Also by 1960, unlike malapportionment at the state level, more often than not the board-of-supervisor system of representation had come to be relatively unbiased as it affected the political parties or else it favored the Democrats. For example, projections based on the 1965 election results show that in Onondaga County had the Democrats polled 50 percent of the total vote, they would have won exactly that portion of the board seats. In Monroe County they would have won 51.2 percent of the seats; in Oneida, 54.0 percent; in Rockland, 60 percent; in Westchester, 66.7 percent; and in Albany, 79.5 percent.[1] Only where there were no cities, with their generous allotment of wards, were the Democrats disadvantaged. Thus in Suffolk County the projection for 1965 shows that had the Democrats won 50 percent of the vote, they would have won only three (30 percent) of the board seats. In contrast to the state level, then, the inauguration of equal apportionment did not necessarily benefit the Democrats although in Suffolk County such certainly was the case.

## Systems of Representation

*The Options*

In the wake of the U.S. Supreme Court's decision in *Baker* v. *Carr,* plaintiffs began to challenge New York's traditional system of county government, and in 1966 a Federal district court issued the first ruling that that system, as it existed in Suffolk County, was unconstitutional.[2] Yet it was one thing to say that the traditional system of representation had to go; what was to replace it was another question, one which occupied the calendars of state and federal courts during the late 1960s and early 1970s.

The most obvious alternative for the counties was the creation of a county legislature based on single member districts, and this was the alternative favored by good government groups such as the League of Women Voters. It was an option chosen by 20 counties in all, including eight of the ten most populous counties. The newly designed county legislatures ranged in size from seven members (Franklin) to 39 (Albany). There was no discernible pattern; the two largest counties, Suffolk and Erie, created legislatures of 10 and 20 members, respectively, while the much smaller counties of Oneida and Dutchess designed legislatures of 30 and 35 members, respectively. There were, of course, partisan consequences associated with these choices. A small number of districts could easily result in minority-party voter strength being canceled out; a large body not only would not have this effect but would offer more officeholding opportunities to party activists.

There were, however, two other alternatives to the traditional board-of-supervisor system, ones which did not represent so complete a break with the past. One of these was a system of at-large, multi-member districts. Such systems of representation have been commonplace in the United States at the state and local government level, and in New York in the 1960s they presented a means whereby a county could retain at least some towns and/or cities as the unit of representation in a county legislature. Thirteen counties, including such relatively populous counties as Rockland, Rensselaer, Schenectady, and Ulster, chose the multi-member district option. Rockland was most perfectly suited for this alternative, since the county had only five towns, and the population of each was such that legislative members could be apportioned in sufficiently perfect multiples to satisfy the Court's standard of equality. Thus the smallest town was given one representative, the second smallest two representatives, and the other three towns four, five, and six representatives, respectively. Other counties opting for multi-member districts were not so fortunate; they were able to maintain the integrity of only a portion of their town or city boundaries.[3]

The other option seized upon by counties in New York was by far the most innovative, and it helped to earn for the state the title of "the redistricting laboratory of the nation."[4] That option was weighted voting, a system of representation under which the board of supervisors was retained intact, but with the difference that now at the periodic board meetings each board member, rather than casting one vote each, would cast votes weighted to reflect his or her unit's population. Rockland County, for example, could have retained its board of supervisors by having each of the five supervisors cast one, two, four, five, and six votes, respectively—although, as explained below, this simple formula came to be challenged in the courts. The 24 counties which chose to convert to a system of weighted voting (several others used it briefly on an interim basis) argued that the board-of-supervisor system was essentially sound since it allowed the natural communities of towns and cities to be represented at the all-county level and since it allowed town-level expertise to be brought to bear on county problems. It was further argued that the alternative of a separate legislature added still another level of office holders to an already cluttered ballot, that it introduced the expense and self-aggrandizing tendencies that all separate organizations invariably entail, and that every ten years its district lines had to be redrawn.

Helping to alert counties to the option of weighted voting was the example of Nassau County.[5] As far back as 1917 Nassau had adopted weighted voting for its board of supervisors as a means of coping with that county's especially uneven population distributions among its several towns and cities. As modified the following year, Nassau's system of weighted voting remains basically intact to this day and, hence, served as an example for other counties to follow. Another example which may have been influential was the report of Governor Rockefeller's Citizen Committee in 1974. That committee had recommended that the county be retained as the basic unit of representation for the state Assembly and that population differences be taken into account by a system of weighted voting which the committee styled "fractional voting." Under the proposed scheme, each county would have continued to have at least one Assembly member (some urban counties several times that number), but Assembly members from the sparsely populated counties would have been able to cast only fractions of votes in the Assembly. Disapproval by the federal district court prevented this plan from being implemented.[6]

Despite the arguments in favor of weighted voting and the precedents for this form of representation, local chapters of the League of Women Voters fought against the adoption of these schemes. In the League's view, the problems of county government, at least in the more populous counties, were too complex and time-consuming to be entrusted to supervisors whose primary responsibility was to look after town interests. (For this reason, too, the League opposed the adoption of Rockland's multi-member district scheme since as part of this scheme the five town supervisors were to be allowed to run as candidates for the county legislature.) Another argument raised by opponents of weighted voting was that such a scheme assumed a very narrow view of the role of an elected representative. This narrow conception was attacked by the federal district court in 1965 when it rejected New York's proposal for a "fractional voting" Assembly. The court noted that "legislators have numerous important functions that have nothing directly to do with voting: participation in the work of legislative committees and party caucuses, debating on the floor of the legislature, discussing measures with other legislators and executive agencies, and the like."[7] Subsequently, the New York Supreme Court in a case involving Herkimer County made the same point. Citing the fact that in the scheme under review one supervisor would cast 45 votes while another would cast five votes, the court wondered whether the one supervisor would be "permitted to make nine times as many speeches, nine times as many telephone calls, and have nine times as much patronage," or in a committee whether he would have "nine times as much power."[8]

In approving weighted voting the New York courts have either ignored these arguments completely or not deemed them to be of overriding importance. The dismissal of the argument regarding legislative committees is especially serious since knowledge of the legislative process in the United States would lead us to expect county legislative committees to play an important role in determining legislative outcomes. Indeed, one of the reasons that Westchester County abandoned its brief experiment with weighted voting was that the committee system was seen as nullifying the reform which the change from the traditional supervisor system was intended to bring about.[9] It is significant that when weighted voting schemes have been considered in New York State and elsewhere, the small towns, not the large ones have been the enthusiastic supporters despite the small number of votes they are allotted.[10] In the eyes of experienced political actors, then, the disporportionate allocation of "person power" which weighted-voting schemes allow in committees and elsewhere appears to be a feature of considerable importance. The legislator's role of ombudsman, or provider of various services to constituents, is also ignored in weighted-voting schemes. The number of constituents clamoring for a board member's services presumably affects the qualities of services which the member can provide, yet the member-constituent ratio varies enormously under weighted voting.

## Partisan Consequences

All of the arguments for and against weighted voting, or for and against multi-member district schemes, were presented in plaintiffs' and defendants' briefs before the courts. But these arguments usually had nothing to do with the motives of the litigants, motives which led to the cases being brought to court in the first place, sometimes at the cost of thousands of dollars in legal fees. For both sides the dominant motive was partisan advantage.

In many counties the prospect of the board of supervisors being abolished in favor of a single-member-district legislature posed a threat to the dominant position of the majority party. Such a legislature would allow the minority political party to capitalize on its pockets of support and elect at least some legislators at every election. In contrast, both weighted-voting schemes and multi-member schemes lump together large numbers of voters into large units of representation, and a bare majority (or even plurality) in

**Table I.** Proportionality of Seats and Votes* Under Three Types of Election Systems

|  | Erie County (Single Member) | | | Rockland County (Multi-Member) | | | Nassau County (Weighted Voting) | | |
|  | % Dem. Vote | % Dem. Seats | Diff | % Dem. Vote | % Dem. Seats | Diff. | % Dem. Vote | % Dem. Weighted Votes | Diff. |
|---|---|---|---|---|---|---|---|---|---|
| 1975 | 55.6 | 60.0 | 4.4 | 60.2 | 88.9 | 28.7 | 44.0 | 3.8 | 40.2 |
| 1977 | 52.7 | 50.0 | 2.7 | 56.9 | 77.8 | 20.9 | 41.7 | 3.8 | 37.9 |

*Two-party vote only (see chapter five, note 11).

a unit will award all that unit's representation to the dominant party. To be sure, in a multi-member system it is theoretically possible for some candidates to be elected from one party and other candidates from another, yet the strong tendency is for all of a unit's several members to be elected from the same party.[11] Under both weighted-voting and multi-member-district systems, therefore, there is a high likelihood that the minority party's proportion of weighted votes or (in multi-member systems) seats won will be far below its proportion of the total vote polled by its candidates. Table I illustrates this property of the two systems, by comparison with single-member-district systems, using examples from three of the most populous counties employing, respectively, the three types of systems. It will be seen that the disproportionalities in representation are greatest in the weighted and multi-member systems.[12] From the examples in the table it can also be understood why in Nassau County the Democrats fought against weighted voting and the Republicans defended it while in Rockland County the situation was precisely the reverse—the Democrats defended the multi-member district system while the Republicans opposed it.

The partisan and other political consequences of the different types of election systems could clearly be seen in the contrast during the 1970s between Nassau County with its board of supervisors and neighboring Suffolk County with its 18-district legislature. In the one there was one-party (Republican) domination; in the other there as a competitive party system where Democrats had a good chance of winning many seats and where they actually won majority control in 1975. In the one there were no additional offices added to the political opportunity structure; in the other there were 18 additional offices created, and as of 1983 three of the state's 34 congressional representatives (one Republican, two Democrats) in Washington had begun their political careers in one of these slots. In Nassau, board meetings were short and featured little or no debate; in Suffolk, legislative sessions were long, often rowdy, and received wide press coverage. Finally, there was a noticeable difference in responsiveness to public pressures articulated in petitions and delegations sent to legislative sessions. In Suffolk the legislature enacted resolutions or local laws in response to organized group demands concerning abortion, Vietnam, atomic power plants, the nuclear freeze, and bottle litter whereas in neighboring Nassau the board of supervisors was able to ignore comparable groups pushing for action on these subjects. There seemed little doubt that the different structure of legislative representation was responsible, at least in part, for all of these conspicuous differences.

## Weighted Voting: The Concept of Legislative Power

Since 1918 political leaders in Nassau County have recognized that weighted-voting schemes are more complex than first meets the eye. In that year the weights on the county's board of supervisors were adjusted, giving the largest town, Hempstead, eight votes, the two smaller towns two votes each, and the city of Glen Cove one vote. When Long Beach was incorporated in 1922 that city also was given one vote. Since Hempstead Town contained 56 percent of the county population, the allotment of 8 of 14 votes, or some 57 percent, might have seemed appropriate. From another perspective, however, the arrangement was seen as totally unreasonable.

Eight votes constituted a board majority; Hempstead was thus in a position to get whatever it wanted and to block whatever it did not want. Said another way, although the town was given only 57 percent of the votes, it possessed 100 percent of the *power*. Supervisors from the other towns were quick to grasp this reality, and they threatened not to attend board meetings. The situation was finally resolved in 1936 when the county drew up its own charter. The charter provided that supervisors from each of the five units would be awarded votes in the ratio of one vote for every 10,000 population. However, to avoid giving Hempstead 100 percent of the power, the provision was inserted that once the votes had been allotted and the number needed for a majority determined (half the votes plus one), Hempstead's allotment of weighted votes would then be reduced to exactly one vote less than that number. Hempstead would now need at least one ally to get its way on the board although by itself it could block a majority from being formed. This curious provision operates in Nassau County to this day.

Although the early political leaders in Nassau had been able, intuitively, to grasp the distinction between a town's *vote* share and its *power* share, it was not until the 1960s that this distinction was formalized by John Banzhaf III in an article provocatively titled "Weighted Voting Doesn't Work."[13] Not only did Banzhaf demonstrate, as had the Nassau supervisors, that vote shares and power shares are not necessarily synonymous, but also he presented a method by which a legislative member's power could be calculated. The method can easily be illustrated. Consider a three-member board, two members representing districts of 20,000 and casting two votes each, and one member, representing a district with a population of only 10,000, allowed to cast only one vote. There are eight possible combinations of yea/nay votes, as shown in Table II. The underlined votes are the "decisive" votes, that is, the votes which if switched (from yea to nay, or nay to yea) would change the outcome of the roll call (from passage to defeat, or defeat to passage). It will be seen from the first column that each board member is able to affect the outcome in four of the eight possible combinations. Stated another way, of all the decisive votes (a total of 12) each member has one-third. Each member may thus be said to exercise 33 percent of the "power," even though the proportions of weighted votes are 40 percent, 40 percent, and 20 percent. The second column in the table presents the power scores if a

**Table II.** Weighted Voting in a Three-Member Legislature

| Member No. of Votes | Weighted Voting Majority Requirement | | | | | Weighted Voting ⅔ Requirement | | | | |
|---|---|---|---|---|---|---|---|---|---|---|
| | A 2 | B 2 | C 1 | Votes in Favor | Outcome[a] | A 2 | B 2 | C 1 | Votes in Favor | Outcome[b] |
| | Y | Y | Y | 5 | P | Y | Y | Y | 5 | P |
| | Y | Y | N | 4 | P | Y | Y | N | 4 | P |
| | Y | N | Y | 3 | P | Y | N | Y | 3 | F |
| | Y | N | N | 2 | F | Y | N | N | 2 | F |
| | N | Y | Y | 3 | P | N | Y | Y | 3 | F |
| | N | Y | N | 2 | F | N | Y | N | 2 | F |
| | N | N | Y | 1 | F | N | N | Y | 1 | F |
| | N | N | N | 0 | F | N | N | N | 0 | F |
| Number of Decisive Votes | 4 | 4 | 4 | | | 4 | 4 | 0 | | |
| Percent | 33 | 33 | 33 | | | 50 | 50 | 0 | | |

A decisive vote is underlined.

[a]Three votes needed to determine outcome.

[b]Four votes needed to determine outcome.

two-thirds vote is needed for a bill's passage. It will be seen that, now, two members alone possess all the power, 50 percent each, while the third member has no power at all. In the language of game theory the third member is a "dummy"; there is nothing he can do to affect the legislative outcome.

Banzhaf asserted that in weighted-voting schemes it is usually the large units which are unfairly favored.[14] The implication of Banzhaf's argument, as advanced in both his article and his *amicus curiae* briefs before various New York courts, was clear: if weighted voting was to be used—Banzhaf did not take a position on its use one way or the other—a fairer method would be to assign weights in such a way that legislators' power shares (rather than weights) were made proportional to population shares. In 1967 New York's highest court, the Court of Appeals, accepted Banzhaf's argument. In its decision *Iannucci* v. *Board of Supervisors*[15] the court ruled that counties could adopt weighted voting schemes provided they could show, through computer analysis, that a supervisor's share of the power, calculated in the way Banzhaf suggested, was proportional to his unit's share of the population. If simple proportional weights (e.g., one vote per 10,000 population) did not yield a satisfactory match-up, then the computer consultant would have to adjust the assigned weights until they did.

The New York Court of Appeals thus ushered in the era of computerized weighted voting, agreeing with Banzhaf that simple weighted voting "doesn't work." It was a remarkable decision, standing as one of the most conspicuous examples ever recorded of a judicial decision based squarely on the findings of scholarly research. But did the court thereby articulate a more realistic view of the representation process? Did it realize the full implication of its ruling? Or, to paraphrase Banzhaf, has computerized weighted voting "worked" any better than the simple weighted voting which it replaced? The answer to these questions is largely in the negative.

## New York's Problems with Weighted Voting

As the discussion of Table II revealed, the Banzhaf method for calculating a legislator's power score rests on the assumptions that each legislator acts independently and that on any roll call all legislators are equally likely to cast either a yes or a no vote. No predetermined party preferences, and hence no partisan coalitions or voting blocs, are contemplated. The Court of Appeals in *Iannucci* accepted this obviously unrealistic assumption, holding that "the sole criterion" by which a legislator's power could be measured was "the mathematical voting power which [he] possesses in theory."

*Unit Domination*
One consequence of the Appeals Court refusal to recognize the possibility of legislative coalitions is that in weighted-voting schemes a few of the larger units can easily possess all the power. In Seneca County, for example, two of the ten towns, representing between them about half of the county population, are awarded 201 and 189 of the 749 votes. Although each town's supervisor is calculated to wield, by the Banzhaf method, 28.5 percent and 21.9 percent, respectively, of the power, by joining together as a voting bloc the two towns can wield over half of the votes and thus can increase their joint power score from 50.4 percent (28.5 + 21.9) to 100 per-

cent, making the other eight towns "dummies." The likelihood of only a few units dominating increases as the unevenness of population distribution increases. Altogether, of the 24 counties using weighted-voting schemes as of 1980 there were four in which as few as one-fifth of the units could dominate and another 18 where the proportion was one-third or less.

*Modified Schemes*

The problem of unit domination may become especially acute in counties which have adopted so-called "modified" weighted voting. These are schemes in which a particularly populous town or city is able to elect one or more additional at-large supervisors to share in the casting of the unit's allotment of votes—each of the unit's representatives now casting one-half, one-third, etc. of the unit's total allotment. Five counties have adopted this approach, although the reasons for their doing so have never been clearly articulated and the number of "extra" representatives assigned to the larger units has followed no fixed ratio formula.

A major problem with modified schemes has stemmed from the fact that the *Iannucci* decision spoke only in terms of a board *member's* power, not in terms of a *unit's* power, and thus directed later courts to look exclusively at member power scores. Of course, so long as each unit has but one member, a member's power and his unit's power are the same; but under the modified schemes the two measurements are not the same. For example, the *Iannucci* decision cited as an example of an unacceptable scheme one which would allot a board member 60 percent of the votes since that share would constitute 100 percent of the power. But what about a scheme which allots a unit's several representatives a combined 60 percent of the votes? Would this be acceptable to the court? Presumably it would.

Nassau County clearly illustrates the problem; and since this county is the largest in the state outside New York City, it is a problem of considerable political consequence. With only five units— three towns and two cities—one unit, the Town of Hempstead, is awarded 70 votes on the county board, just under the 71 required for a legislative majority. However, these 70 votes are divided 35 each between Hempstead's two supervisors, an arrangement which began in 1918. When the New York Supreme Court and later the

Court of Appeals came to evaluate the Nassau scheme in terms of the *Iannucci* guidelines, Hempstead's allotment of 70 votes was seen to yield 54.6 percent of the total board power, a proportion which was virtually equal to the town's population share (56 percent) and hence judged by the courts to be appropriate. The court arrived at the 54.6 percentage by adding together the power scores of the two Hempstead members, each of whom as an individual member was calculated, by the Banzhaf method, to wield 27.3 percent of the total power of the six-member board. However, had there been but one Hempstead supervisor casting the total allotment of 70 votes on a five-member board, the power of the Town of Hempstead would then have been calculated as possessing 88.9 percent of the power, and the scheme would have been ruled unconstitutional. Thus the modified scheme, inherited from 1918, gave Hempstead much more power than it would otherwise have been allowed to possess.

Did the Court of Appeals, in handing down the *Iannucci* decision, intend this result? It is difficult to believe that it did. The decision was proclaimed by the court as intended to protect the small units from domination by the larger ones; yet by failing to address the problem stemming from plural representation, as practiced in Nassau as well as in the other four counties, the court achieved precisely the opposite result. The record shows that when the practice of plural representation first began in Nassau in 1918 with the creation of a second post of supervisor in the town of Hempstead, the explicit purpose was to double the number of votes given to the *town;* it was taken for granted that the supervisors would combine their votes into a single bloc. (The fact that both supervisors are invariably from the same political party makes the likelihood of bloc behavior even stronger.) The failure of the New York courts to recognize this history, and to think only in terms of board *members,* is among the ironies of the New York experience.

*Problem of Measurement*
The New York courts' troubles with the Banzhaf power scores are also illustrated by the problem of measuring fairness of apportionment. How exact must be the match-up between population share and power share, and how should the match-up be measured?

As explained in chapter five, for single-member-district schemes and multi-member schemes the normal method of measurement, applied by federal and state courts, has been to find the ideal size district—dividing the total state or county population by the number of members—and then to compare the size of the most populous and least populous districts with the ideal. The two discrepancies are expressed as a percentage of the ideal (e.g., 10 percent too large, 10 percent too small), and the range of discrepancy calculated (20 percentage points). The top half of Table III shows how the New York Court of Appeals, and later the U.S. Supreme Court, applied this method of calculation to Rockland County's multi-member scheme. Both courts found the range of 11.9 percentage points to be reasonable and not excessively large as charged by the plaintiffs.

For weighted-voting schemes the comparable method of measurement identifies the ideal percentage of power which each supervisor should have (i.e., his unit's proportion of the total county population) and then compares that proportion with the power which he is shown to have by the Banzhaf method of calculation. The two most extreme discrepancies are identified (e.g., 10 percent of population, 11 percent of power=10 percent too much power; 20 percent of population, 18 percent of power=10 percent too little power), and the range calculated (20 percentage points).

For the first several years the New York courts adopted this method of determining the constitutionality of the various weighted-voting schemes which were brought to them for review. But then in 1973 the state's highest court rendered a decision which recalls the "mathematical quagmire" of which Justice Frankfurter warned in *Baker* v. *Carr*.[16] In the case of *Franklin* v. *Krause*[17] the Court of Appeals looked only at the *percentage point* discrepancies for each of the two most extreme districts (following our example, one percentage point, and two percentage points) and added them together to find the range (three percentage points); missing from the method was the division to obtain the deviation from the ideal value. In the case at hand, involving Nassau County, rather than find a discrepancy range of over 230 percentage points, which would have rendered the scheme unconstitutional (schemes with a discrepancy range of less than 10 points had been declared unacceptable), the court thus found a discrepancy range of only "7.3%," and accordingly approved the scheme. The bottom half of Table III shows the results obtained by the two methods of calculation.

How had New York's highest court made such a fundamental error in arithmetic? The answer is to be found in the brief filed

**Table III.** Measuring Equality of Apportionment in Multi-Member and Weighted-Voting Counties

|  | ROCKLAND (Multi-Member) | | | | |
|  | No. of Members | Population | Ideal Population* | Difference | Percentage Difference |
|---|---|---|---|---|---|
| Stony Point | 1 | 12,114 | 12,156 | 42 | −0.3 |
| Haverstraw | 2 | 23,676 | 24,312 | 636 | −2.6 |
| Orangetown | 4 | 52,080 | 48,624 | 3,456 | +7.1 |
| Clarkstown | 5 | 57,883 | 60,680 | 2,897 | −4.8 |
| Ramapo | 6 | 73,051 | 72,936 | 1,015 | +0.2 |
|  | 18 | 218,804 | | | RANGE 11.9 |

$* \dfrac{218,804}{18} \times$ No. of members

|  | NASSAU (Weighted Voting) | | | | |
|  | No. of Votes | Percent Power | Ideal Power Share* | Difference | Percentage Difference |
|---|---|---|---|---|---|
| Glen Cove | 2 | 5.6% | 1.8% | +3.8 | +211.1 |
| Long Beach | 3 | 5.6% | 2.3% | +3.3 | +143.5 |
| No. Hempstead | 23 | 13.0% | 16.5% | −3.5 | − 21.2 |
| Oyster Bay | 32 | 20.4% | 23.1% | −2.7 | − 11.7 |
| Hempstead | 35 | 27.3% | 56.3% | −1.7 | − 3.0 |
|  | 35 | 27.3% | | RANGE 7.3 | RANGE 232.2 |

*Percent of county population.

with that court by Nassau County's attorney, one who had been specially hired for the case. It was in that brief, when the case reached its final stage, that the "7.3%" figure first appeared. The court bought the argument whole, thus overlooking the observation of the lower court (which had found the scheme unacceptable) that Glen Cove "had greater than three times its share of power," i.e., over 200 percent too much. The opposing lawyers also failed to spot the error. By the time the error was called to their attention several years later, it was too late; the Court of Appeals refused to rehear the case. It remains to be seen whether the post-1980 litigation will produce a different result.

## Conclusion

Four different systems of representation have been identified in this chapter: (1) single-member-district systems, (2) multi-member district systems, (3) unit systems with each local government or local ward electing one member with one vote, and (4) unit systems with the unit representative(s) casting weighted votes. The first two systems have been approved by the U. S. Supreme Court; the third has been outlawed by that Court; and the fourth, in either its simple-ratio or its computerized "power" formulation, has yet to be judged by the nation's highest tribunal. Each system carries with it different consequences for party competitiveness, for party recruitment, for the power wielded by local government units, and for responsiveness to voter needs and demands. As the post-1980 reapportionment period began, it was clear that these consequences, as well as past judicial inconsistencies, would be the cause of continued litigation.

## Notes

1. The methodology used in these calculations is that used in chapter 5.

2. *Bianchi* v. *Griffing* (1966), 256 F. Suppl., 617.

3. In Greene County 4 of 7 districts coincided with jurisdictional units and in Tompkins County 7 of 12. In the remaining counties using multi-member districts the majority of districts cut across the towns and/or cities.

4. Robert C. Dixon, *Democratic Representation: Reapportionment in Law and Politics,* Oxford University Press (New York, 1968), p. 546. For essays on the introduction of weighted voting in New York see Robert W. Imrie, "The Impact of the Weighted Vote of Representation in Municipal Governing Bodies in New York State," *Annals of the New York Academy of Science,* Vol. 219 (1973), pp. 192–199; and Ronald W. Johnson, "An Analysis of Weighted Voting as Used in Reapportionment of County Government in New York State," *Albany Law Review,* Vol. 34 (1969), pp. 1–45.

5. Other examples of weighted voting are to be found in the New York City Board of Estimate, political party conventions that allow or require bloc voting (e.g., New York State nominating conventions, British Labor party conventions), and the electoral college (where, in practice, all of a state's electoral votes are cast as a bloc).

6. *WMCA Inc.,* v. *Lomenzo* (1965), 238 F. Suppl. 916.

7. *WMCA Inc.* v. *Lomenzo* at 923.

8. *Morris* v. *Board of Supervisors of Herkimer County* (1966) at 454–455.

9. The question of committee power is discussed in *Shilbury* v. *Board of Supervisors* (1967), 284 NYS 2d 124, where the court ruled that boards of supervisors cannot delegate their power; hence committee votes are legally meaningless.

10. See, for example, the observations of William Riker and Lloyd S. Shapley, "Weighted Voting: A Mathematical Analysis for Instrumental Judgment," in J.R. Pennock and J.W. Chapman, eds., *Representation,* Atherton Press (New York, 1968), pp. 199–216; and also of John F. Banzhaf III, whose work is discussed below. Evidence that the small units prefer weighted voting could be seen in Suffolk County in 1978 when the small towns began to urge that the county abandon its legislature in favor of a weighted-voting board of supervisors.

11. In 1975, for example, in all but 2 of the 13 multi-member counties a majority of the districts were captured by candidates of the same party.

12. As in the previous chapter, analysis in the table is based on the two-party vote only. Altogether in 1975 the average size discrepancy for all single member districts (N=18) was 7.7 percentage points, while multi-member counties (N=12) and weighted voting counties (N=22) averaged 14.6 points and 12.5 points, respectively. It should be noted, however, that in both Nassau and Rockland Counties, for the years shown, the minority party would have benefited from similar disproportionalities had the vote totals been reversed. Thus the problem for these two counties is not the problem of bias, as this term was defined in the last chapter, but rather the problem of the enormous advantage which is always enjoyed by the majority party under the respective systems used in these counties.

13. *Rutgers Law Review,* Vol 19 (1965), pp. 317–343.

14. Our simplistic three-member example in Table II is thus misleading (in majority situations). With larger size legislatures, the bias against smaller units becomes evident.

15. 282 N.Y.S. 2d 502.

16. 369 U.S. (1962) 186.

17. 344 N.Y.S. 2d 885.

# 7.

# Parties, Elections, and Representation: A Summary

THREE PERSPECTIVES have guided the preceding analysis of parties, elections, and representation in the state of New York: (1) comparison with other American states, (2) the match-up between reformers' intention and resulting practice, and (3) historical evolution. By way of conclusion to the volume, a summary of the findings is in order.

*New York in Comparative Perspective*
Beginning in the 1970s observers throughout the United States began to decry the fact that American political parties were languishing, that they were no longer the vital institutions they once were. Against this negative backdrop perhaps the most significant comparative theme which emerges from the preceding chapters is that while signs of party demise are evident, the parties in New York continue to be the dominant political groupings in the state.

As organizations, the parties in New York are strong. Their strength is reflected most notably in their ability to control the nominations for most of the important public offices—although no longer those at the statewide level—and also by the fact that the party chairmanship posts with their considerable patronage opportunities are still sources of power. Indeed, it is this latter aspect of party strength which continues to result in voter disenchantment with matters "political"; as of 1982, in the metropolitan area alone there were six county, town, or city chairmen, or former chairmen (Republican and Democrat) who were serving jail sentences or who were appealing convictions on crimes such as extortion, mail fraud, and tax evasion. Within the electorate, too, the parties are strong. The majority of voters continue to choose the option of enrolling in one of the parties, and an extremely closed enrollment system insures that when there is a primary contest, only the long-standing enrollees will participate. In addition, in general elections most voters will follow the party cue when choosing among the many candidates on the ballot. Within the legislature the parties likewise continue to be strong, their members united by self-interest and, to varying degrees, by shared values and a commonality of constituent interests and attitudes. Finally, the parties in New York compete vigorously at the statewide level, making New York one of the most competitive states in the nation.

Taken together, these characteristics allow the parties in New York to perform the important functions for which they are noted in making democratic government work. First, they aggregate the divergent interests and attitudes of the electorate, thereby serving as agents of reconciliation. To capture the governorship or, since the "one man, one vote" reapportionment, to form a majority in the legislature, a party must become less homogeneous and bring together in some minimum degree the diverse policy demands which are typical of the component regions of the state and of the various demographic groupings within them. Second, the parties make the state government at least broadly responsive to voter demands, by identifying one of the parties with the governorship and with the majority legislative party or—when there is split control between the two houses—legislative parties. Although most of the hundreds of bills discussed by the legislature each year are ones with which the parties do not become identified and whose passage or defeat often stems from the efforts of paid lobbyists, voters can always express their general satisfaction or dissatisfaction with the way the state is being run by voting for or voting against the party in control. Without parties this fragile link between the government and the electorate would be greatly weakened, and the power of other organized groups would be enhanced accordingly. Third, the parties in New York continue to be the major recruitment agencies for those seeking public office; the overwhelming proportion of nominees for public office each year are persons who have been active in party affairs, one way or another. Finally, through the loyalties they instill and the organizations they sustain the parties in New York continue to stimulate participation in the electoral process. Without them turnout on election day would drop to even lower levels.

The foregoing generalizations apply only to the two major parties. The three minor parties do not aggregate interests, do not provide a mechanism for responsiveness, and do not recruit many candidates for office. In short, they are better described as pressure groups. The presence of these minor parties makes the New York party system the most distinctive in the nation, and their presence is explained by an election law which is almost equally distinctive, allowing one candidate to be the nominee of more than one party.

Several other items should be listed in this final summary of features which distinguish New York from most other American states: (1) an election law which allows the loser of a party's primary to become the candidate of another party, (2) a so-called "challenge" primary law for statewide office, (3) a ballot format which is labeled "office block" but which closely resembles the party column format, and (4) a wide variety of systems of representation at the local government level.

*Intentions and Results*

The political history of New York has been punctuated with attempts by reformers to change the election law in ways designed to bring about desired goals. A retrospective glance at these reforms leaves little doubt that more often than not those changes have not achieved their desired goals, and many have resulted in unanticipated outcomes.

Perhaps the greatest failures, in light of the hopes of their architects, have been the two historic primary laws—the law of 1913 which introduced the pure primary and the law of 1967 which introduced the challenge primary for statewide offices. The first did not succeed in removing organization control over candidate selection; the second did not succeed in inducing contests between party organization and a challenger. Also conspicuous for their failure have been the various attempts made since the 1950s to increase voter turnout. Although without these reforms turnout might have fallen to even lower levels, the hopes of the reformers that turnout would increase from what it was in the 1950s have not been realized.

Among the unanticipated consequences of electoral reforms, perhaps most noteworthy are those which stemmed from changes in the ballot format. First, the change from the party-column paper ballot to the office-block ballot served to discourage minor party growth while the switch later to voting machines had the opposite result. In neither case was the outcome anticipated. The Wilson-Pakula Law of 1947 likewise had profound consequences for the party system; in this case a law intended to preserve the two-party system turned out to have the very opposite result. The 1976 registration reform should also be mentioned. Intended to increase voter turnout by introducing registration by mail, the new form designed for that purpose called attention to the "independent" option, and thereby resulted in a decrease in the pool of voters available for primary election participation.

No less than legislative decisions, judicial decisions have resulted in consequences which were unforeseen, or at least ones not mentioned by the justices. The most fundamental changes which have resulted from the Federal courts' insistence on population equality for legislative districts have related to political party representation; yet this is a subject conspicuously absent from the courts' written decisions. The New York courts, for their part, have insisted on computerized weighted voting in county government as a means of protecting the smaller towns; in fact that mandate has often led to the very opposite result.

All of the examples cited could be used by those who would argue that legislatures and courts had better abandon their attempts at reform since good intentions are bound to be frustrated by political realities. Others might argue that the record demonstrates that legislative and judicial decisions do have consequences but that the authors of these reforms must take particular care to see that the consequences are the ones intended. For reformers taking the latter, more optimistic perspective, remaining on the reform agenda for the 1980s were three obvious items: elimination of the cross-endorsement system, public financing of elections, and a run-off primary for statewide office. Which leads to the final theme of the volume.

*Historical Development*

The most noteworthy political changes in New York during the period 1950–1980, as identified in the preceding chapters, were (1) the *decline* of voter participation, partisan loyalty, party organizational strength, the comparative electoral significance of New York City, Republican strength, the bipolarity between the partisan preferences of New York City voters and voters elsewhere; (2) the *increase* of primary elections, statewide competition, strength of minor parties, Democratic strength outside New York City, electoral strength of suburbs; and (3) the *introduction* of primary elections for statewide office, easier registration requirements, equal-population legislative districts, a variety of representation systems in local government.

Some of these changes have stemmed from legislative or judicial decisions, others from broad social changes. Both sources of change will continue to influence the nature of parties, elections, and representation in the years ahead. It is hoped that the analysis from the perspective of the early 1980s as presented in the previous chapters will serve as a backdrop against which these future developments can be measured.

# Author Index

**Author Index**

# Subject Index